The Best in Kids

Creative Activities for Preschool Children

by
Barb Borycki
Jo-Anne Sotski-Engele

Photography by Mitch Hippsley
Illustrated by Kendra Roberts

The Best in Kids

Creative Activities for Preschool Children

Third Printing 1994

Canadian Cataloguing in Publication Data
Borycki, Barb, 1955-
The best in kids
Canadian ed.--
Includes index.
I.S.B.N. 0-9693372-0-5
First published by Best In Kids Publishing
1. Creative activities and seat work.
2. Handicraft.
3. Cookery.
I. Sotski-Engele, Jo-Anne, 1961-
II. Title.
GV1203.B66 © 1988   649'.51   C88-098043-5

Published and distributed by
Western Extension College Educational Publishers
A Division of Academic Enterprises Ltd.
Box 110, Saskatoon, Saskatchewan S7K 3K1
Telephone: (306) 373-6399

Printed in Canada
by Consolidated Graphics

Acknowledgements

Val Ziegler – for doing the typesetting, design and layout of our book.

Mitch and Geraldine Hippsley (Photography by Mitch - Yorkton) for their creative ideas in photography.

Kendra Roberts – for her delightful illustrations.

Cindy Swartout –for the use of her home for the photography sessions.

Carpet-Land (Yorkton) – for supplying the paint for the cover photograph.

Thank-you to the following children for participating in the photography sessions.

> Scott Benko
> Courtney Borycki
> Mark Borycki
> Brock Engele
> Carly Hippsley
> Braydon Marianchuk
> Kristina Swartout
> Whitney Swartout

Thank-you to Rochelle Bondarenko (age 5) for doing the printing on cover title.

Thank-you to our husbands Tom and Barry for their unending patience and support throughout our endeavor.

Forward

Welcome to "The Best In Kids!" Our book was written for parents of preschool children. The idea for our book evolved through our experience of working with the parents of young children. We found that parents were very concerned about the skills their children needed to acquire in order to be successful at school. Although we both feel that we should "let our children be children," we found that parent concerns were very genuine and also very appreciated from a teacher's viewpoint. We feel that although parents should never pressure their children into learning what "we" want them to learn, there are very unstructured, fun methods in which to build skills necessary for that time when children reach school age.

Hence the creation of "The Best In Kids." The important thing that we want to stress is to allow your child the freedom to create and imagine without interfering with the learning process. Your job is to supply and create the material and atmosphere conducive to creative learning. Let your child do things his way – not yours.

We have included a special section on teaching your child the alphabet and numbers. Your child may begin to ask about letters or numbers; that would be the time to use the activities in this special section.

Our wish for you is to have fun, and always enjoy your child. Always remember their childhood may be short but their memories will last a lifetime.

Table of Contents

Dedication

We would like to dedicate this book to our children Brock, Courtney and Mark. By doing the activities in this book, we hope to give you the joy that you have given us . . . just by being our children.

 inter onders

FINGERPLAYS AND SONGS

Five Little Snowmen
(This Little Pig - use fingers and toes)
Five little snowmen happy and gay
The first one said, "What a beautiful day"
The second one said, "We'll never have tears"
The third one said, "We'll stay here for years"
The fourth one said "What will happen in May"
The fifth one said, "Look, we're melting away"

Winter Activities
(tune: Mulberry Bush)
Here we go walking in the snow, in the snow, in the snow
Here we go walking in the snow, on a winter morning
This is the way: 1. We make a snowman
                      2. Make an angel
                      3. Skate around
                      4. Ride a sled
                      5. Use our skis

Snowflakes
Snowflakes whirling all around, all around, all around
(Flutter fingers high above head, in the air, slowly falling to ground)
Snowflakes whirling all around
Until they cover all the ground

Variation: Have your child pretend he's a snowflake, twirl and fall to the ground.

7

The Melting Snowman

Five little snowmen, knocking at the door
One melts away and then there were four
Four little snowmen playing with me
One melts away and then there were three
Three little snowmen playing with you
One melts away and then there were two
Two little snowmen playing in the sun
One melts away and then there was one
One little snowman, when the day is done
He melts away, and then there is none

Mittens

Slide your fingers into the wide part
*(Hold right hand forward, palm down,
fingers together, thumb apart)*
Make your thumb stand alone and tall
*(slide left hand over grouped fingers
and then over thumb)*
When you put your mittens on
You won't feel cold at all

My Zipper Suit

My zipper suit is bunny brown *(point to clothes)*
The top zips up, the legs zip down *(draw fingers up and down)*
I wear it every day
My mommy bought it from uptown
Zip it up, zip it down *(zip up, and down)*
And hurry out to play *(run on spot)*

Making A Snow Man

Roll it, roll it, get a pile of snow, *(roll arms)*
Rolling, rolling, rolling, rolling, rolling, here we go
Pat it, pat it, face it to the south *(pat hands on lap)*
Now my little snow man's done, eyes and nose and mouth *(point to
facial features)*

Come Sing A Song of Winter

(tune: The More We Get Together)
Come sing a song of winter, of winter, of winter,
Come sing a song of winter, the cold days are here.
With winter winds blowing and rosy cheeks glowing,
Come sing a song of winter, the cold days are here.

Here's A Hill

Here's a hill *(make hill with left arm)*
All covered with snow
We'll get on our sled
And ZOOM! Down we'll go *(Swoop right hand downward)*

Here's A Chimney

Here is a chimney *(tuck thumb in fist)*
Here is the top *(other hand on top of fist)*
Take off the lid *(remove hand)*
Out smoke pops *(pop up thumb)*

The Snowman and The Bunny

A chubby little snowman *(make a fist)*
Had a carrot nose *(poke thumb out)*
Along came a bunny
And what do you suppose? *(other hand – make rabbit ears)*
That hungry little bunny
Looking for his lunch *(bunny hops around)*
Ate that snowman's carrot nose *(bunny nibbles at thumb)*
Crunch, crunch, crunch

ARTS AND CRAFTS

Stars and Snowflakes

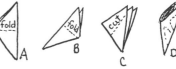

Materials: paper
scissors
glue
glitter (optional)

Square your paper. Leave the paper folded so that it is a triangle. Fold the paper in half (A.) Fold the triangle in half again (B). Cut along a very slanted line (C). Open the paper and you have an eight pointed star.

Variation: To make a snowflake cut designs along each edge. Have child spread glue and decorate with glitter.

Variation: Use coffee filters to make snow flakes. Leave unfolded and dip various corners in food coloring.

Hint: To square a paper, fold one corner to the opposite edge. The two edges of the paper should meet evenly. Cut off the leftover part.

Outdoor Snow Sculpture

Materials: paint
        paint brush

Have your child build a sculpture out of snow. Anything will do. Give him some paint and let him decorate it.

Mittens

Materials: construction paper
        yarn
        crayons
        scissors
        glue

Have your child make a pair of mittens by laying his hands on colored construction paper while you trace around them. Have him make designs with crayons. Glue or staple yarn to each mitten.

Winter Scenes

Materials: construction paper
        white paint
        cotton balls
        glue

Have your child paint a white hill on a large piece of blue paper and add cottonball snowmen to the hill.

Variation: Paint with white glue. Sprinkle white powder detergent over glue for wintery effect.

Winter Fingerpainting

Materials: blue, purple, white fingerpaint (use cold colors, one or more)
tin foil

Fingerpaint with cold colors on tinfoil for a chilling effect.

Winter Whipped Soap Snow

Material: white paper
crayon or paint
liquid soap (Ivory)

Have child crayon or paint a picture. Whip liquid soap until very stiff with electric mixer. Add ""snow" to drawing by painting with whipped snow. Adds 3-D effect. Excellent after a fresh snowfall.

Snowman

Materials: construction paper   glue
cotton balls   scissors

Pull apart cottonballs to make head, and body of snowman. Glue onto blue construction paper. Make construction paper, eyes, nose, hat, button, broom and scarf, etc. Be creative: make eyes from cheerios, macaroni mouth, fruit loop nose and button coat, etc.

Honeycomb Snowflakes

Materials: Honeycomb cereal
dark construction paper
glue

To make a snowflake design, glue Honeycomb cereal on dark construction paper or glue edges of Honeycomb cereal together to make snowflake design.

Doily Snowmen

Materials: doilies
dark construction paper
markers, scrap paper, cereal, etc.
glue

Paste doily on dark construction paper. Make face out of markers or scraps.

Hint: Make clean up time hassle free. Paste a picture of your child's favourite animal on a wastebasket with "FEED ME" printed on it. Ask your child to "feed the dog" when cleaning up.

GAMES

Angels

(one child or more)

Make angels in the snow. Have your child lay flat on his back moving arms and legs back and forth.

Memory Game

(one player)

Have your child repeat a series of numbers or words.

Opposites

(one player)

You say a word, and have your child say the opposite.

Clapping Game

(one player)

Clap a rhythmic pattern for your child. Have him reproduce the pattern.

Drama

(one player)

Have your child act out a description of various words such as large, short, tired, etc.

Observation

Great party game *(one or more players)*

Place any small items on a tray. Cover them with a cloth. Uncover the tray and let your child look at them for 30 seconds. Cover up the tray. Have your child tell you what was on the tray. (Start off with 3 objects and increase as your child gets better.)

Fox and Geese

(2 or more)

This is a good game to play in the snow. Trample down a circle about twenty feet in diameter. This makes a wheel. Trample down 6 spokes. The fox chases the geese in and out and around the patch. Geese may jump across from one spoke to another but the fox may not. Any goose tagged by the fox is fox for next turn.

RECIPES

Frosty the Snowman

Stack two scoops of vanilla ice cream
on a plate. Sprinkle on coconut. Add
a gumdrop hat and chocolate chip
eyes, nose and mouth.

Fancy Snowballs

2 tbsp.	soft butter	30 ml
1 cup	icing sugar	250 ml
1 cup	peanut butter	250 ml
1 cup	rice krispies	250 ml

Combine ingredients and roll into small balls. Dip in icing made of
icing sugar and water. Roll in fine coconut, ground nuts, cake
sprinkles, crushed smarties, crumbled cookies, etc. Use your imagination!

Snowball Popcorn Balls

1 cup	light corn syrup	250 ml
1/2 cup	sugar	125 ml
1 tbsp.	vinegar	15 ml
1 tbsp.	butter	15 ml
1 tsp.	vanilla	5 ml

Combine sugar, syrup and vinegar. Stir until sugar is dissolved over
medium heat. Add butter and boil without stirring to soft crack stage.
Add vanilla. Pour taffy over popcorn and stir from the bottom of the
bowl with a fork. When taffy cools a bit grease hands and work quickly
to form balls. Wrap each ball in plastic and store in a cool dry place.
Make a face on the balls with gumdrops. (see photograph)

Soft crack: Mixture forms thread like spun glass when it hits the water.
Thread will break when pressed, (132°-143°C or 270°-290°F)

Snow Cap Eggnog

2	eggs	2
1 cup	milk	250 ml
1/4 cup	sugar	60 ml
1/2 tsp.	vanilla	2 ml
2 tbsp.	vanilla ice cream	30 ml

Beat eggs, milk, sugar and vanilla in bowl. Pour into glasses and top
with a spoonful of ice cream.

Hot Chocolate

1/2 cup	boiling water	125 ml
1 cup	milk	250 ml
1 tbsp.	cocoa	15 ml
1 tbsp.	sugar	15 ml
1/2 tsp.	vanilla	2 ml
	marshmallows	

Pour 1/2 cup water into a measuring cup and microwave for 1 minute. Add the boiling water to 1 cup of milk. Add other ingredients except marshmallows to the milk, and stir. Place milk in microwave and cook for 1-1/2 minutes. Take out and stir. Top with marshmallows.

Old Time Molasses Pull Toffee

1-1/2 cups	brown sugar	375 ml
1/2 cup	water	125 ml
1/2 cup	molasses	125 ml
2 tbsp	vinegar	30 ml
1/4 tsp.	cream of tartar	1 ml
1/8 tsp.	baking soda	1/2 ml
3 tbsp.	butter	45 ml

Time for some toffee!

Mix sugar, water, molasses and vinegar and cook until mixture boils. Add cream of tartar and continue cooking until the mixture is brittle. (Very important!) Hint: Drop a tiny bit into a cup of water and if it hardens you know it's ready. When nearly cooked, add the butter and soda. Grab your boots, coat and family, and rush outside to find a clean piece of snow. Pour onto the snow in strips. Enjoy!

BOOKS

Burton, Virginia Lee. *Katy and the Big Snow*
Delton, Judy. *Three Friends Find Spring*
Duvoisin, Robert. *White Snow, Bright Snow*
Hader, Berta and Elmer. *The Big Snow*
Keats, Ezra Jack. *The Snowy Day*
Pamall, Peter. *Alfalfa Hill*
Peterson, Hans. *The Big Snowstorm*
Shortall, Lonard. *Country Snowplow*

Hint: When reading a story to your child, have him tell you what is happening in the picture.

Sweet St. Valentine's

FINGERPLAYS & SONGS

How Many Valentines?
Valentines, valentines
How many do you see?
Valentines, valentines
Count them with me
One for father *(hold up thumb)*
One for mother *(hold up pointer)*
One for Grandma too *(hold up middle man)*
One for sister *(hold up ring finger)*
One for brother *(hold up pinky)*
And here is one for you! *(make heart shape with thumbs and pointer fingers)*

Jack Frost's Valentine
(tune: Yankee Doodle)
Jack Frost made me a valentine
So lacy edged and bright
He left it on my windowpane
As he passed by last night
I cannot read the message
It's written very fine
But I'm sure in Frostland speech
It's "Be My Valentine"

My Valentines

(tune: Farmer in the Dell)
I have a little valentine
That someone sent to me
It's pink and white and red and blue
And pretty as can be

Snowman Valentine

(tune: London Bridge)
We made a snowman yesterday, yesterday, yesterday
We made a snowman yesterday
In round and fat design
We pinned a red heart to his chest, to his chest, to his chest
We pinned a red heart to his chest
And called him Valentine
Optional: Play "Pin the Heart" on the snowman

Valentine's Day

Here comes the postman
Tis Valentines Day
He's bringing to me *(point to self)*
Five letters today *(hold up 5 fingers)*
I'll open them quickly *(pretend to open letters)*
And what will I see?
Five pretty hearts *(hold up 5 fingers)*
Just for me! *(point to self)*

Valentine Song

(tune: London Bridge)
I've a secret, I've a secret
And I'm hiding it away
I'm just waiting for the morning
Of St. Valentine's Day
Oh, you'll like my little secret
And I think it's very fine
And it says I'm choosing someone
For my own Valentine

My Valentine

(tune: The Farmer in the Dell)
My Valentine is red
I made it just for you
I drop it in the mailbox
And mail it on to you
The mailman picks it up
And sends it on to you
And then you open it to find
It says "I love you true"

Valentines Red

(tune: Lavender's Blue)
Valentines red dilly dilly
Valentines green
When I am King dilly dilly
You shall be Queen
Valentines pink dilly dilly
Valentines blue
All seem to say dilly dilly
That I love you

Valentine Song

(tune: Camptown Racetrack)
You're a special friend of mine, friends, friends
You're a special friend of mine
Yes, you are
And I think you're very fine, very, very
And I think you're very fine
Be my Valentine

ARTS & CRAFTS

Textured Valentine

Materials: paper
ribbon
scissors
buttons
glue
gummed seals, etc.
macaroni

Cut valentine shape and paste interesting materials in pleasing designs.

Valentine Plant

Materials: paper cup
              scissors
              popsicle sticks
              foil
              glue
              red and green construction paper

Cover paper cup with foil. Glue a heart and leaves to a popsicle stick. Insert the stick into the bottom of the paper cup.

Heart Mobile

Materials: red, white, pink construction paper
              string or yarn
              scissors
              glue
              crayons
              newspaper

Child cuts out hearts of various sizes from construction paper. Glue hearts onto a long piece of string or yarn. Decorate hearts. Hang in window.

Valentine Person

Materials: red and white construction paper
              glue
              scissors
              crayons

Make hearts of various sizes for head, body, hands and feet. Arms and legs are strips of red and white construction paper, accordian folded. Add features with crayon. Be creative! Ask your child what is missing. Maybe a hat, hair, whatever. Have fun!

Use these valentines in other arrangements to make your childs favourite animal. (cat, mouse, fox, butterfly, lovebugs, etc.)

Helpful Hint: If you have trouble with paint sticking to a particular surface, mix it with a little glue.

Valentine Mouse

Materials: red construction paper

            spaghetti   scissors

            corn seed   yarn

            glue

Cut a red paper heart. Fold in half. Use spaghetti for whiskers, corn seed for the eye and yarn for the mouse's tail.

Toothpick Valentine

Materials: red construction paper

            toothpicks

            scissors

            glue

            crayons

            glitter, sequins, buttons, macaroni, etc. (optional)

Cut out two hearts the same size. Glue toothpicks on one heart and cover with the other heart. Use crayons to draw eyes, nose and mouth.

Rose Colored Glasses

Materials: pipe cleaners

            red or pink cellophane

            construction paper

            glue

Have your child cut out two hearts that will fit over their eyes. Glue pink or red cellophane on each side. Attach pipe cleaners for each ear piece. Your child can tell stories of how the world looks through rose colored glasses.

Fingerpaint Valentines

Materials: red finger paint

            white paper

            scissors

            glue

Fingerpaint with red. Cut the fingerpaint sheets into heart shapes. Decorate the large red heart with small white heart shapes and hang in window.

Valentine Hat

Materials: red construction paper
          long cardboard tube

Starting at one end of the tube, cut 1/2 inch-wide strips, stopping each strip about 3 inches from the other end of the tube. Spread all the strips out slightly to make a hat which will fit your head. Cut red construction paper hearts and glue them all over the hat from bottom to top.

Valentine Flower

Material: paper plate
          scissors
          glue
          red and green
          construction paper

Cut out small valentines to glue on paper plate in shape of a flower. Use green construction paper for stem and leaves.

Yarn Valentines

Materials: construction paper
          yarn
          glue

On a sheet of construction paper glue heart shapes to make a design or a creature. Outline the hearts with glue and press yarn into the glue.

Valentine Watch

Materials: construction paper
          white glue or stapler
          pen

Make a watch from construction paper. Glue (or staple) strip to fit over wrist. Cut out the valentine shape to glue to strip with numbers on it. Attach two construction paper hands with a fastener in the center.

Frosty Valentines

Materials: red construction paper
              Q-tips
              white glue
              salt, sugar or clean white sand

On large red heart shapes, draw designs with Q-tips and white glue. Sprinkle with salt, sugar or clean white sand.

Valentine Card

Materials: red construction paper
              white construction paper or doily
              picture of your child

Fold red construction paper. Cut out a white heart (or use white doily) and paste on front. Print verse:

> *Someone loves you,*
> *Do you know who?*
> *Take a look inside and see*
> *The one who loves you is me*

Inside paste a picture of child. (Use pre-school picture or poloroid picture.)

GAMES

Valentine Game

(tune: London Bridge)
(five or more)
Will you be my Valentine? Valentine? Valentine? *(one child runs around and stops in front of another child)*
Will you be by Valentine? Sweet Valentine
Yes, I'll be your Valentine, Valentine, Valentine *(second child answers)*
Yes, I'll be your Valentine, Sweet Valentine
Come and be our Valentine, Valentine, Valentine *(they hold hands and run around in a circle together while everyone sings)*
Come and be our Valentine, Sweet Valentine

Postman Hunt

(2 or more)
Instead of just giving your child his valentines; hide them. Have your child play postman and find the valentines. It will be far more exciting receiving Valentines this way.

Helpful Hint: Valentine stamping is fun! Make heart shaped valentines from styrofoam, dip the shapes in red tempera and paint.

Racing Hearts

(4 or more)

Divide into two teams (one line may work, non-competitive). Place large paper hearts at intervals on the floor in front of each team. The first player in each team runs to the other end of the room and back, stepping on each heart as he runs. The team completing the action first, wins.

Catching Cupid

(3 or more)

Players are all blindfolded except for "me". He is "Cupid". A small bell (optional) is fastened around his wrist. He may move around play area as he wishes. The blindfolded players try to catch Cupid by listening to his bell. When a player catches him, the two exchange places. Parent or parents should be there to be sure the blindfolded children don't bump into anything.

don't peek !

Valentine Game

(tune: Where Oh Where Has My Little Dog Gone)
(5 or more)

Oh where oh where is my Valentine?
Oh where oh where can it be?
Oh where oh where is my Valentine?
Oh where oh where can it be?

Oh here oh here is my Valentine
I'm walking with him now
I'm walking with my valentine
I'm walking with him now

Five or more children form a circle. A child walks around the circle looking for a Valentine. He then chooses a child and they walk (or run) around together while everyone sings.

Mr. Postman

Mr. Postman, who is blindfolded, sits on a chair. Put a valentine under the chair. A child tries to take the valentine so the Postman can't hear him. If he gets the valentine without the Postman tagging him, he may be the Postman.

Valentine's Dance

(tune: Skip To My Lou)

1. Who will be my Valentine?
   Who will be my Valentine?
   Who will be my Valentine?
   I love you my darling

2. I will be your Valentine . . . .
3. Make a circle two by two . . . .
4. Walk around two by two . . . .
5. Jump up and down two by two . . . .
6. Skip around two by two . . . .
7. Swing your arms two by two . . . .
8. Tip toe around two by two . . . .

(use your imagination and carry on!)

Newspaper Valentine

Provide children with newspaper. Ask them to close their eyes and tear out a valentine from newspaper.

RECIPES

Strawberry Swing

1 cup	milk	250 ml
1 tbsp.	strawberry jam	15 ml

Blend together the milk and the strawberry jam. Pour into glass. Enjoy!

Fun Fudge

1-6 oz. pkg.	chocolate tidbits	
1-6 oz. pkg.	butterscotch tidbits	
1 can	Borden's Eagle Brand Sweetened Condensed Milk	
1 cup	chopped nuts	250 ml
1/2 tsp.	vanilla	2 ml

Melt chocolate and butterscotch tidbits with sweetened condensed milk in a double boiler or over very low heat. Stir constantly until "bits" melt. Remove from heat. Add chopped nuts and vanilla. Spoon the chocolate mix onto foil or wax paper. Chill in refrigerator until firm.

Helpful Hint: Cut sponges into different sized heart shapes. Sponge paint red and pink hearts on white heart shaped paper.

Cinnamon Toast

2	slices toast	2
	margarine or butter	
1/8 cup	white confectioner's sugar	30 ml
1/8 cup	brown sugar	30 ml
1/2 tsp.	cinnamon	2 ml

Toast bread and spread with butter or margarine. Mix sugars and cinnamon. Sprinkle mixture on toast.

Valentine Finger Jello

1-6 oz. pkg.	red jello	
2 pkgs.	Knox gelatin	2
1 cup	hot water	250 ml
1-1/2 cup	cold water	375 ml
	whipped cream (optional)	
	gumdrops or strawberries (optional)	

Dissolve jello in hot water. Stir thoroughly. Dissolve Knox gelatin in 1 cup of cold water. Combine red jello and gelatin. Add 1/2 cup cold water to mixture and stir. Pour into a shallow pan such as a jelly-roll pan to chill. When jelled, cut the jello into heart shapes with a cookie cutter. Use an aerosal can of whipped cream to decorate the edges. Garnish the center with a red gumdrop or a whole strawberry.

BOOKS

Bulla, Clyd Robert. *The Valentine Cat*
Cohen, Miriam. *Bee My Valentine*
Haywood, Carolyn. *A Valentine Fantasy*
Hopkins, Lee Bennet. *Good Morning To You Valentine*
Schweninger, Ann. *The Hunt for Rabbit's Galosh*
Skorpen, Liesel Moak. *Plenty For Three*
Wahl, Jan. *Pleasant Fieldmouse's Valentine Trick*

Helpful Hint: Make "Hearty" sandwiches: cookie cut bread into heart shapes. Spread with red jam.

St. Patrick's Day Delights

FINGERPLAYS AND SONGS

For St. Patrick's
(tune: London Bridge)
1. All the ants have worn green pants
   Worn green pants, worn green pants
   All the ants have worn green pants
   For St. Patrick's
2. All the cats have worn green hats
3. All the ewes have worn green shoes
4. All the pigs are dancing jigs
5. All the yaks have worn green slacks

Five Little Leprechauns
Five little leprechauns knocked at my door *(hold up five fingers)*
One chased a rainbow, then there were four.
Four little leprechauns, oh so wee *(hold up four fingers)*
One picked a shamrock, then there were three
Three little leprechauns hiding in my shoe *(hold up three fingers)*
One found a toadstool then there were two
Two little leprechauns dancing in the sun *(hold up two fingers)*
One went in search of gold, then there was one
One little leprechaun on the run *(hold up one finger)*
He shined his shoe buckles, then there was none *(hold up fist)*

I'm A Tree

I am a tall tall tree *(stretch up tall, arms high above)*
I spread my branches for all to see *(put arms to side)*
I feel cold on a windy day *(wrap arms around self)*
I bend, I nod and how I sway! *(do as words suggest)*

Happy St. Patrick's Day

Five little leprechauns dressed in green
They're the happiest I've ever seen
This leprechaun has a big gold ring
This leprechaun has a song to sing
This leprechaun wears a funny wig
This leprechaun likes to dance a jig
This leprechaun nods his head to say
"We wish you a happy St. Patrick's Day"
(start with a fist - then put one finger up at a time, then wave "Bye, Bye")

Did You Ever See A Froggie?

(tune: Did You Ever See A Lassie)
Did you ever see a froggie, a froggie, a froggie *(child sits on haunches)*
Did you ever see a froggie just sit in the sun?
Now jump my little froggie, oh froggie, oh froggie, *(child does frog jumps)*
Now jump my little froggie and let's have some fun
Now swim my little froggie, oh froggie, oh froggie *(child pretends to swim)*
Now swim my little froggie in water so clear
Now sit my little froggie, oh froggie, oh froggie
Now sit my little froggie on your haunches right here *(child sits on haunches)*
Now sleep my little froggie, oh froggie, oh froggie *(child pretends to sleep)*
Now sleep my little froggie right here in the sun
Wake up now little froggie, oh froggie, oh froggie *(wake up and hop around)*
Wake up now little froggie and let's have some fun

St. Patrick's Green

(tune: Yankee Doodle)
St. Patrick's Day is with us
The day when all that's seen
To right and left and everywhere
Is green, green, green!

26

Elfman

I met a little elf-man *(use thumb and pointer finger to show small)*
Down where the lilies blow
I asked him why he was so small *(shrug shoulders, put hands out - palms up)*
And why he didn't grow
He slightly frowned and with his eyes *(tilt head to side, looking serious)*
He looked me through and through
"I'm just as big for me" said he *(place hands on hips)*
"As you are big for you"

Little Green Frog

"Gung, gung" went the little green frog one day
"Gung, gung" went the little green frog
"Gung, gung" went the little green frog one day
And his eyes went "aah, aah, gung"
(fingers around eyes, stick out tongue)

ARTS AND CRAFTS

Potato Head Leprechaun

Materials: construction paper
           glue
           scissors

Have the patterns drawn for your child. Have him cut out the patterns (or do it yourself) and glue them together. Have your child name his leprechaun.

Leprechaun Hats

Materials: green construction paper
           glue
           scissors

1. Fold 12 x 18 inch green construction paper to form a triangle.
2. Draw a diagonal line from that center to each upper corner of the triangle. Cut along the two lines.
3. Fold and paste down the triangle flap.
4. Curl the pasted peak with scissors.
5. Let your child put on his hat.

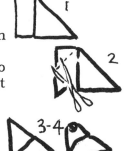

Potato Prints

Materials: knife
            paper
            pencil
            green paint
            potato
            jar lid

Cut a potato in half. Pour some thick paint into a jar lid. Take one of the potato halves and scratch a simple design in the center of the cut side of the potato. Use the tip of a spoon to scoop out the parts around the design. Have your child dip the design into green paint. Press the design onto the paper. (To avoid having your child use too much paint, have him press the design onto paper towel before pressing onto paper).

You can also print with a grapefruit, lemon, orange, onion, pepper or cabbage.

The Irish Touch

Just Like Magic!

Materials: green crayon
            green construction paper
            white paint
            paint brush

Draw a design with green crayon on green paper. When finished brush thin white paint over the paper. Lines will appear from nowhere, showing the previously hidden object!

Shamrock Man

Materials: construction paper
            scissors
            glue
            crayons

Cut out a shamrock on green paper. Decorate the shamrock to look like a person. Add hat, hands, shoes and facial features.

Shamrock

Materials: white paper
            green crayon
            glue

Draw large shapes on paper.
Color and cut out pieces.
Glue on leaf to each side of stem.

GAMES

Leprechaun Leap

(3 or more players)
Players lineup one after another. The first player in line squats down. The second player in line puts his hand on the squatting player's back and leaps over the first player. The third player leaps over the both of them, and so on.

St. Patrick's Day Sardines

(3 or more players)
This is a good game to play indoors where there are plenty of hiding places. One player is chosen to be the first sardine (pull straws). The other players leave the room and slowly count to twenty (you can help them count) while the sardine hides. Then they all begin to hunt for him. The first one to find him hides in the same place, quickly and quietly. The next player to find the two of them hides there too. But when they do they don't tell anyone else. The game continues until everyone is hiding in the same place. The person who first discovered the hiding place becomes the next sardine.

RECIPES

Green Shakes

1 can (6 oz.)	frozen lemonade	168 g
1 cup	milk	250 ml
2 cup	vanilla ice cream	500 ml
1 cup	water	250 ml
	green food coloring	

1. Pour juice, water and milk into blender. (If you don't have a blender put in a quart jar and shake.)
2. Scoop in 2 cups ice cream.
3. Cover in blender at high speed for 30 seconds. (see photograph)

St. Patrick's Cheesecake

Pan: 9" x 13"
1. Crumb mixture: Crush 18 thin chocolate wafers.
   Mix 4 tbsp. (60 ml) melted butter.
   Pack into pan.
2. Take 2 packages lime jello (small)
   Mix with 3 cups (750 ml) boiling water
   Cool till egg white consistency.
   Beat well.
3. Whip 1 cup (250 ml) whipping cream (dream whip can be used).
4. Mix whip cream and jello mixture.
5. Add 1-1/2 cups (375 ml) miniature marshmallows.
6. Add 1 cup (250 ml) creamed cottage cheese that has been through the blender.
7. Mix well. Spread over crumbs. Refrigerate.

You may add green maraschino cherries and green food coloring if you wish.

Stuffed Celery

	cheese spread	
1	celery stick	1
2 tsp.	sunflower seeds	10 ml

Fill celery with cheese spread. Sprinkle with sunflower seeds.
Variation: Use peanut butter and sprinkle with raisins.

Puff Pudding

1 package	instant pudding	1 package
1 cup	miniature marshmallows	250 ml

Mix pudding according to directions on the package. Add marshmallows. Chill.

Note: Before gelatin was invented, people made puddings thick by using Irish Moss they found along the seashore.

BOOKS

Balian, Lorna. *Leprechauns Never Lie*
Bunting, Eve. *St. Patrick's Day in the Morning*
Calhoun, Mary. *The Hungry Leprechaun*
Cantwell, Mary. *St. Patrick's Day*

E aster scapades

FINGERPLAYS AND SONGS

Benny Bunny
Hippity hop, hippity hop *(have child bounce around like a bunny)*
Here comes Benny Bunny
Fuzzy and white
Furry and bright
Bouncy Benny Bunny

Funny Bunny
Here is a bunny with ears so funny *(hold with right hand up, two bent fingers)*
And here is a hole in the ground *(make a hole with thumb and forefinger on left hand)*
If a noise he hears
He pricks up his ears *(straighten fingers in right hand)*
And jumps in his hole in the ground *(jump fingers into the hole)*

Little Bunny Rabbit
Oh, little bunny rabbits
With funny little tails
And ears so long you seem to me
Like boats with furry sails
You nibble at your cabbage
Your ears go flippy flop
Then, all at once you turn away
And hop, hop, hop
Tape a cotton ball tail to child's backside. Make bunny ears out of construction paper, fold ends and tape to head. Do actions to verse.

Easter Treats

Chocolate bunnies and candy eggs
Are in the stores today
They must mean that Eastertime
Is not too far away

If I Were A Bunny

(tune: Farmer In the Dell)
If I were a bunny
I'd tell you what I'd say
"Howdy folks, hello to you
And Happy Easter Day"

Bunny

(tune: Yankee-Doodle)
I'm a bunny with a bushy tail
I carry eggs in my pail
Some eggs are pink
And some are blue
They are pretty
And so are you.
Hippity-Hippity, hop, hop, hop, hop
Hippity-Hippity, hop hop
Hippity-Hippity, hop, hop, hop, hop
Hippity-Hippity, hop, hop
(child may like to pretend to be the Easter bunny)

Funny Bunny

(tune: Row Your Boat)
Funny, funny, funny bunny
Hopping down the road
Funny, funny, funny bunny
My, you have a load

Funny, funny, funny bunny
Won't you stop and see
Funny, funny, funny bunny
If there's an egg for me?

Helpful Hint: After reading a story to your child ask him to recall specific details.

Helpful Hint: Talk about other little animals that hop (grasshoppers, frogs, birds, kangaroos, etc.)

ARTS AND CRAFTS

Paper Bag Bunny

Materials: white paper bag   cotton ball
           string or yarn   scissors
           newspaper   paint and brush
           construction paper

Stuff two bags, one smaller for head. Attach paper arms, feet and ears. Attach string or yarn around the neck. Paint on a face. Stick on a cottonball for the tail. (see photograph)

Paper Bunny

Materials: paper   toothpicks
           scissors   glue
           cotton balls (pulled apart)

Make 2 circles for bunny head and body, and have your child fill in by gluing on cotton balls. Toothpicks make good whiskers. Add facial features. (see photograph)

Bunny Necklace

Materials: spool
           cotton balls
           yarn
           construction paper
           white glue
           scissors

Cover a spool with cotton. Cut two ears from construction paper. Cover with cotton balls and glue to top of cotton covered spool. Make a loop from yarn and push the glue end into the hole in the top of the spool. (see photograph)

Egg Pictures

Materials: construction paper
           crayons
           glue

Have your child cut out construction paper eggs of various colors and sizes. Use them to create Easter animals and scenes (bunny, chicks, lambs, flowers, etc.) Crayoned details can be added to complete the pictures.

Helpful Hint: Make your own gift wrapping paper. Have your child select one color of paint to use in developing a pattern on a large sheet of plain newsprint. Wrap a special gift.

Easter Bunny Car from an Egg Carton

Material: paper egg carton
glue or paper fasteners
paint
construction paper
tin foil
scissors
Saran wrap
marshmallows
toothpicks

First paint the whole carton with paint. (Leave the carton closed). Then cut away a piece of the cover over the third row of egg holders. This makes the seat for a driver and one passenger. The wheels are made by tracing around a small glass to make construction paper circles. Use metal foil for hub caps and bumpers. Fasten on wheels with glue or paper fasteners. A small sheet of saran wrap will make the windshield. Marshmallow Easter bunnies with toothpick ears can sit in the car. (see photograph)

Easter Baskets

Materials: plastic container   construction paper (optional)
cotton balls   glue

Glue cotton balls all around the container. (Pastel colored cotton balls look terrific). Make the basket with or without a handle. (see photograph)

Glistening Eggs

Materials: colored construction paper
thick tempera paint
salt

Your child may cut out egg shapes from colored construction paper. Then paint designs on the eggs using thick paint and sprinkle the designs with salt while the paint is still wet. When egg is dry, the design is repeated on its reverse side.

Waxed Paper Eggs

Materials: light colored crayons
scissors
waxed paper
iron
newspaper

Crayon shavings are placed between two layers of waxed paper. These are then ironed at a low setting, between sheets of newspaper. When cool, cut into egg shapes. These translucent eggs may be hung or mounted onto narrow brightly colored paper frames.

Peter Cottontail

Materials: styrofoam cup
styrofoam ball
cottonball
construction paper
white glue
scrap ribbon
scissors

Attach the ball to the cup with white glue. Glue ribbon at the base and bow at neck. Cut a slit across the back of the head near the top. Cut out two ears and slip the ears into the slits. Make a tail from cotton and glue at the back of the cup. Add construction paper features.

Decorating Easter Eggs

Materials: hard boiled eggs
colored yarn
torn tissue paper
colored scraps
felt pens
white glue
scissors

Have your child rub paste or white glue on shells of hard boiled eggs, then glue on bits of colored yarn, torn tissue paper or crushed, colored egg shells.

Variation: You could also have your child decorate the eggs with different colored felt marking pens.

Easter Chicks

Materials: styrofoam egg carton cup
2 cotton balls
yellow and orange construction paper
white glue

Stuff cotton balls into styrofoam egg cup to form a chick. Make features (eyes, beak, feet) from yellow and orange construction paper. Glue onto cotton to make your Easter Chick.

Stand-Up Rabbits

Materials: toilet tissue roll
construction paper
cotton ball
scraps of material or felt, stickers, crayons, etc.

Cover toilet tissue roll with colored construction paper or leave white. Add features: eyes, nose, mouth, ears, whiskers and tail using any materials you have on hand and glue onto toilet tissue roll.

GAMES

The Bunny Hop

Dance the bunnyhop! (Ray Anthony, *Bunny Hop*, Capitol)

Egg Carton Bean Race

(2 players or more)
Materials: egg cartons   paper cup
           beans   straw
Put a bean in each cup of the egg cartons. Your child has to pick up the beans by sucking them through the straw, and dropping them into a cup.
Variation: If more than one person is playing, each person goes until they drop a bean.

✗ Spoon Race

(2 players or more)
Materials: boiled egg
           spoon
Place an egg on a spoon. Have your child walk to a certain point and back again without dropping the egg. If there is more than one child see who can carry it the furthest without dropping it.

Easter Rabbit

(tune: Yankee Doodle)
(4 or more)
A furry Easter Rabbit
Jumping up and down
Takes a friend and they hold hands
Hopping all a-round!
The children form a circle and sing this tune as they play. One child is chosen to stand inside the circle to be the first "Easter Rabbit." The "Easter Rabbit" jumps up and down as children sing first two lines of song. When the children sing "take a friend" the "Easter Rabbit" chooses a child and they hold hands and hop around inside the circle. The game continues with the children singing the song and each "Easter Rabbit" choosing a friend until all the children are chosen.

Helpful Hint: Let your child pretend to be an Easter Bunny delivering eggs to different people.

36

Treasure Hunt

(1 or more players)
Hide chocolate eggs around room. Have your child find them.

RECIPES

Peter Rabbit Salad

Materials: lettuce leaf
            pear half
            raisins
            regular marshmallows or almonds
            cherry
            cottage cheese

Place a pear half on a lettuce leaf. Add raisins for eyes. Marshmallow bits or almonds for ears, a cherry for a nose and cottage cheese for his tail.

Egg Nog Pops

2 cups	vanilla ice cream	500 ml
16 oz. can	frozen orange juice	500 ml
1	egg	1
1-1/2 cup	milk	375 ml

Mix first three ingredients together. Gradually beat in milk and pour into popsicle molds. Freeze.

Pretzel Bread

Great for Easter morning!

1 pkg.	yeast	1 pkg.
1 cup	warm water	250 ml
1 tsp	salt	5 ml
1 tbsp.	sugar	15 ml
4 cups	flour	1 litre
1	egg beaten	1
	coarse salt	

Dissolve the yeast in warm water. Add the salt and sugar. Blend in the flour. Knead dough until smooth. Cut into small pieces. Roll into ropes and twist into pretzel shape. Place on lightly greased cookie sheet. Brush with beaten egg. Sprinkle with coarse salt. Bake immediately at 425°F (220C) for 12-15 minutes.

Variation: For hard pretzels use only 1-1/4 cup (300 ml) flour and 1/4 cup (50 ml) melted butter. Shape smaller and bake until brown.

Helpful Hint: Have children decorate eggs with crayons and then dye them with food coloring.

Caramel Candied Popcorn

7 quarts	popped corn (without salt)	7
2 cups	salted peanuts	500 ml
1 cup	almonds	250 ml
1 cup	butter or margarine	250 ml
2/3 cup	corn syrup	165 ml
2 cups	brown sugar	500 ml
1 tsp.	vanilla	5 ml
1/2 tsp.	baking soda	2 ml

Bring butter, syrup and sugar to a boil. Boil for 5 minutes without stirring. Remove from heat and add 1 tsp. vanilla and 1/2 tsp. baking soda. Pour over popcorn mixture and put in big roaster. Bake for 1 hour at 250° stirring every 15 minutes.

Funny Sandwiches

Spruce up your child's lunch with fancy sandwiches! Use steel cookie cutters to cut out rolled out bread. Fill the sandwiches with your child's favourite filling. Use olives, pickles, cherries, etc., to make faces or designs. (i.e. doughnut cutter, gingerbread man)

Candy Bunny

2 large marshmallows
2 chocolate chips
1 miniature marshmallow
toothpicks (colored are nice)
construction paper
1 egg white
icing sugar

Make "glue" from beating the egg white and adding icing sugar until mixture is thick and fluffy. Then glue the large marshmallows forming the head and body. Chocolate chips are then glued for eyes. Use the toothpicks to make whiskers and use construction paper to make bunny ears and glue them in place. The miniature marshmallow tail can be attached to complete your candy bunny.

BOOKS

Brown, Margaret Wise. *Home For a Bunny*
Brown, Margaret Wise. *The Runaway Bunny*
Friedrich, Priscilla. *Easter Bunny That Overslept*
Gackenbach, Dick. *Mattie Rabbit*
Parish, Peggy. *Too Many Rabbits*
Provensen, Alice & Martin. *Who's in the Egg*
Tresselt, Alvin. *The World in the Candy Egg*
Zolotow, Charlotte. *The Bunny Who Found Easter*

Spring **S**urprises

FINGERPLAYS AND SONGS

Spring Has Come

The melting snow says, "Drop, drop, drop"
The little frog says, "Hop, hop, hop"
The little bird says, "Peep, peep, peep"
The little vine says, "Creep, creep, creep"
The little bee says, "Hum, hum, hum"
The little flower says, "Spring has come"

The Robin Song

(tune: London Bridge)
Listen to the robins' song
Spring is here and winter's gone
I must find a friendly tree
For my little wife and me
We will build a cozy nest
Grass and mud and string are best
Soon we'll have a family
Baby robins, one, two, three

The Old Man

It's raining, it's pouring *(move hands up and down like rain)*
The old man is snoring *(make snoring sounds)*
He went to bed *(bend head to pretend to sleep)*
And bumped his head *(rub head)*
And couldn't get up in the morning *(bend head again to pretend to sleep)*

Little Froggie

(played like: This Little Piggy Went to Market)
This little froggie broke his toe
This little froggie said, "Oh, oh, oh"
This little froggie laughed and was glad
This little froggie cried and was sad
But this little froggie so thoughtful and good
Ran for the doctor as fast as he could

Eentsy Weentsy Spider

The eentsy, weentsy spider went up the water spout *(make circles out of thumbs and forefingers - put tips together - twist upward)*
Down came the rain and washed the spider out *(wiggle fingers while moving downward - push outward)*
Out came the sun and dried up all the rain *(make a big circle with arms over head)*
And the eentsy, weentsy spider went up the spout again *(make circles out of thumbs and forefingers - put together - twist upward)*

Spring Song

(tune: London Bridge)
Little ducks go quack, quack, quack
Quack, quack, quack,
Quack, quack, quack
Little ducks go quack, quack, quack
In the springtime.

Little lambs go baa, baa, baa
Baa, baa, baa
Baa, baa, baa
Little lambs go baa, baa, baa
In the springtime
Continue using your own animal sounds. (bees, cows, chicks, kittens, puppy, etc.)

A Little Hole

Dig a little hole *(dig)*
Plant a little seed *(drop seed)*
Pour on a little water *(pour)*
Pull a little weed *(pull up and throw away)*

Chase a little bug *(chasing motion with hands)*
Heigh-ho, there he goes *(shade eyes)*
Give a little sunshine *(cup hands)*
Let it grow, grow, grow, *(smell flower, eyes closed, smiling)*

Umbrella

I put up my umbrella
On a rainy day
My umbrella keeps me dry
When I work and play

Pitter Patter

Pitter-patter *(let fingers patter on floor, table, hand, etc.)*
Pitter-patter
Listen to the rain!
Pitter-patter
Pitter-patter
On the window pane!

Beehive

Here is a beehive, Where are the bees? *(make a fist)*
Hidden away where nobody sees *(cover eyes)*
Watch and we'll see them come out of the hive
1, 2, 3, 4, 5 *(pop out each finger, one at a time)*

Gray Squirrels Bed

In a little hole *(make a circle with pointer finger and thumb)*
In the trunk of a tree
A little gray squirrel
Was as cozy as could be *(cuddle self)*
The Northwind blew *(wave arms)*
Snowflakes sailed around *(flutter fingers)*
But little gray squirrel
Slept very sound *(pose as sleeping)*

The Coming of Spring

(tune: Farmer In The Dell)
There is something in the air
That is new and sweet and rare
The scent of many summer things
A whirl as if of wings
There is something too that's new
The color of the blue
That is in the morning sky
Before the sun is high

Helpful Hint: Save old newspapers to allow your child to paint on.

Helpful Hint: Talk about sounds heard in spring. (birds, raindrops, breezes, rustling trees, etc.)

ARTS AND CRAFTS

Popcorn Blossoms

Materials: popcorn
             brown paint or crayon
             glue
             construction paper

Have your child draw branches on a sheet of paper. Paste popped corn on them. Eat and work at the same time!
optional: Use a real branch

Bag Kites

Materials: paper bag
             scraps of yarn, gift wrap, etc.
             glue   yarn

Have your child take a bag and add construction paper or gift wrap scraps, yarn, pieces of cloth, etc. Add a yarn handle and a cloth tail. Then run outdoors and feel resistance as the bag fills with air.

Sail Boats

Materials: blue construction paper
             white paper triangles
             colored paper rectangle
             glue

Give your child a blue sheet of construction paper and have him draw wavy watery lines on it. Give him 4 or 5 sizes of white paper triangles for sails and a colored paper strip for boats. Paste to background.

Baking Cup Flower

Materials: baking cup
             glue
             green construction paper

Glue a baking cup onto a sheet of construction paper. Have your child rip out a stem and leaves from construction paper. Use small pieces of construction paper for the ripping.

Rainbow Jars

Materials: sand, pebbles, shells, seeds, macaroni, dried beans, coffee
             grounds, popcorn kernels, twigs, beads, buttons, cotton
             balls   empty jar

Go on an outdoor exploring trip to collect materials. Separate the materials into piles or small dishes. Fill in the jar with layers of materials.

Paper Pinwheels

Materials: heavy construction paper
            straw
            crayons
            straight pin

Cut out a complete square. Draw the lines from each corner to the middle. Cut along with scissors. Now bend (don't fold) the points marked a, b, c, d to the middle dot and tape. Push a straight pin through the center of the small cardboard circle and into the straw. Blow and watch it spin.

*Wrap tape around pointy part of pin so that it won't poke anyone.

GAMES

Sailboat Puddle Race

Materials: paper
            straw
            toothpick
            plasticine or clay
            bottle cap or jar lid

Cut out a paper sail. Poke a toothpick through the sail. Put a little lump of clay in a bottle or cap of jar lid. Push the toothpick into the clay. Take your child outdoors and find a puddle. Use a drinking straw to blow the boat across the water.

Buzzing Bee

Have a buzzing contest with your child. Take a deep breath and see who can buzz-z-z-z-z-z-z the longest.

Giggle Game

See who can make the other laugh. On signal turn and face each other. Each tries to make the other laugh by making faces.

Memory Game

Give your child a category and have him name all the things he can think of (i.e.) fruits, vegetables, toys, boys names, girls names, nursery rhymes, body parts, colors, pieces of furniture.

RECITES

Spring Basket Cupcakes

Push a pipe cleaner into a cupcake to
make a handle. Then add gumdrop flowers.
(see photograph)

Flowerpot

Fill a paper cup with ice cream.
Stick in a lollipop for a flower.
(see photograph)

Taco Snack

1 small bag of taco chips
1 cup shredded cheddar cheese (250 ml)
On a large plate place the taco chips and sprinkle cheese over them.
Cook in microwave for 25 seconds.

Fudgsicles

3 oz. pkg.	chocolate pudding (not instant)	85 g
3-1/2 cups	milk	875 ml
1 cup or less	sugar	250 ml or less

Prepare pudding according to directions, but substitute 3-1/2 cups,
(875 ml) milk. Blend until smooth. Pour into popsicle molds. Freeze.

Circus Clown Cone

Put a scoop of ice cream in an ice cream cone. Turn the cone upside
down on a plate. Use chocolate chips or gumdrops to make the face
on the ice cream. (see photograph)

*Variation: Give your child an icecream cone. Have him decorate with
chocolate chips, cherries, candied sprinkles, coconut, etc.*

BOOKS

Baun, Arline and Joseph. *One Bright Monday Morning.*
Carle, Eric. *The Very Hungry Caterpillar.*
Hoban, Lillian. *Sugar Snow Spring.*
Klein, Leonore. *Mud! Mud! Mud!*
Krauss Ruth. *The Carrot Seed.*
McCloskey, Robert. *Make Way For Ducklings.*
Scheer, Jullian, and Bileck, Marvin. *Rain Makes Applesauce.*
Yashima, Taro. *Umbrella*

izzling
ummer

FINGERPLAYS AND SONGS

Once I Saw A Beehive

Once I saw a beehive *(make a beehive with both hands)*
Out in the maple tree *(point)*
I said "Little Honeybee *(hold hands to mouth)*
Come out and play with me!"
"Bzzzzz! went the honeybees *(emphasize the Bzzzz!)*
Inside the hive! *(make beehive again)*
And then they came out
One, two, three, four, five!" *(show one finger at a time)*

The Lesson

I splash – I flop *(wave hands to make splashing motion)*
I tread – I hop *(hop up and down)*
My arms go in a spin *(make circles with arms)*
My legs are kicking up and down *(kick legs)*
Then suddenly – I swim! *(pretend to swim)*

Anthill

Once I saw an ant-hill *(make ant hill with both hands)*
With no ants about *(shake head)*
So I said "Dear little ants
Won't you please come out?"
Then as if the little ants
Had heard my call
One, two, three, four, five came *(pop out each finger, one at a time)*
And that was all!

My Garden

This is my garden *(extend one hand forward, palm up)*
I'll rake it with care *(make raking motion with other hand)*
And then some flower seeds *(make planting motion with thumb)*
I'll plant in there.
The sun will shine *(make circle above head with hands)*
And the rain will fall *(let fingers flutter down to lap)*
And my garden will blossom *(cup hands together, extend upward slowly)*
And grow straight and tall.

Kick A Little Stone

(tune: Farmer In The Dell)
When you're walking by yourself
Here's something nice to do
Kick a little stone and watch it hop ahead of you

The stone is round and white
It's shadow round and blue
Along the sidewalk, over cracks
The shadow bounces, too

Skipping Susan

(tune: Merrily We Roll Along)
Little Susan learned to skip
Skip and skip, skip and skip
Round and round her rope did skip
Skip and skip and skip and skip

Little Susan learned to hop
Hop and hop, hop and hop
We thought that she'd never stop
Hop and hop and hop and hop

Little Susan stretched up tall
Stretched and stretched and stretched and stretched
Then she made herself so small
Smaller, smaller, smaller, small

Little Susan goes to sleep
Sleep and sleep and softly sleep
As the stars begin to peep
Sleep, sleep, so softly sleep

Rain

(tune: London Bridge)
The rain is raining all around
It falls on field, and on the trees
It rains on all the umbrella's here
And on the great big ships at sea

Movements

(tune: Mary Had A Little Lamb)
1. This is how (worms all squirm) (3)
   This is how the worms all squirm
   And birdies fly like this
2. Spiders crawl right (up the wall) (3)
   Spiders crawl right up the wall
   And elephants walk like this
(Do actions to song)

The Little Turtle

There was a little turtle (show "little" thumb and pointer finger)
He lived in a box (make box shape with hands)
He swam in a puddle (make swimming motion)
He climbed on the rocks (lift leg and arms to pretend to climb)
He snapped at a mosquito   (open hand as you extend
He snapped at a flea   arm, then quickly pull arm
He snapped at a minnow   back and close hand)
And he snapped at me (make snapping motion and point to self)
He caught the mosquito   (bring closed
He caught the flea   hand to
He caught the minnow   mouth)
But he didn't catch me (shake finger and head)

Thistle-Seed

(tune: I Love Little Pussy)
Thistle-seed, thistle-seed
Fly away, fly!
The hair in your body
Will take you up high
Let the wind wheel you
Around and around
You'll not hurt yourself
When you fall to the ground
(child can do the actions)

Animals

We'll hop, hop, hop like a bunny
And run, run, run like a dog
We'll walk, walk, walk, like an elephant
And jump, jump, jump like a frog
We'll swim, swim, swim like a goldfish
And fly, fly, fly like a bird
We'll sit right down and fold our hands
And not say a single word
(do actions to verse)

Five Little Ducklings

One little duckling, yellow and new
Had a fuzzy brother and that made two
Two little ducklings now you can see
They had a little sister and that made three
Three little ducklings - will there be more?
A friend came along and that made four
Four little ducklings went to swim and dive
They met a little neighbor and that made five
Five little ducklings, watch them grow
They'll turn into fine big ducks you know

ARTS AND CRAFTS

Thumbprint Bugs

Materials: ink pad or felt pen
          paper/crayons
Have your child look at his thumb and tell you what he sees. He'll be surprised to see the lines and whorls. Ask your child to make his thumbprint on a piece of paper. Add eyes, legs, antennae and wings with crayons.

Chalk Walk

Materials: colored chalk
Your child will love this activity!
Give him a piece of chalk and have him decorate your sidewalk with a picture. A good rain will wash it away!

Helpful Hint: Tell your child what season it is. Talk about the changes that happen in summer.

Pleat and Dye Prints

A great outdoor activity.

Materials: containers (3)
food colouring (blue, red, yellow)
newspaper
paper towels (white)
water

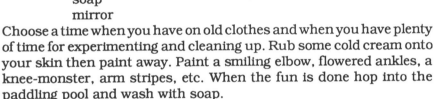

Pour a little of each food color into different containers. Add a little water to each color. Pleat the paper towel the long way and the short way. Hold the paper towel in the middle. Dip a corner into one of the food colors. (The color spreads quickly, so take the towel out quickly.) Dip a second and third corner into each color. Unfold the towel carefully and lay it on a newspaper to dry. Use it as gift wrap.

Body Painting

Materials: tempera paint
cold cream
brush
water
newspaper
washcloth
soap
mirror

Choose a time when you have on old clothes and when you have plenty of time for experimenting and cleaning up. Rub some cold cream onto your skin then paint away. Paint a smiling elbow, flowered ankles, a knee-monster, arm stripes, etc. When the fun is done hop into the paddling pool and wash with soap.

Wet Watercolors

Materials: tempera paints
drawing paper
brush
pan of water
newspaper
pencil or pen (optional)

Soak a piece of drawing paper in water. Hold it up to drip for a few seconds. Place the wet paper on newspaper. Paint on wet paper. The colors will blend together and blur as you paint. When the painting is dry, you can use a pen or pencil to draw a picture over the painting.

Helpful Hint: When the weather is nice, take advantage of it and do as much as possible outside. The fresh air is great!

Mud Art

Material: mud
             bucket of water
             sticks and mud mushing tools
             cardboard or wood scraps

Mix up some mud and spread it, glob it, or pile it on a piece of cardboard. Add designs with fingers, sticks, wood blocks, spoons or any other tools. Press pebbles, grass, feathers, etc., into your picture for details. Have fun!

Paint With Bubbles

Materials: 1/2 cup ivory flakes
              1/2 cup water
              bowl
              electric or hand mixer
              food coloring
              paper for painting
              newspaper
              a few small containers

Whip the ivory flakes and water until thick and stiff. Put "fluff" into cups or containers. Add food coloring to make the colors you'd like to use. Mix. Cover work area with newspaper. Paint a picture on your painting paper using your fingers. Let the picture dry overnight.

Painted Glue

Materials: white glue
              waxed paper
              marking pens or tempera paint
              toothpick

Spill glue onto waxed paper, in odd shapes, and poke a toothpick through. Let glue dry until hard and clear. Color the dried glue with markers or paint. Remove the shapes from the paper. Hang them in windows, from mobiles or even around your neck. Hint: Glue takes about 3 days to dry.

Rock Sculpture

Materials: smooth rocks or pebbles
              epoxy glue
              marking pens or acrylic paints
              scraps and objects for adding detail

Turn a rock into something special by:
- gluing rocks together with epoxy glue;
- decorating with seeds, string, buttons, felt, foil, bottle caps, flowers, etc.
- add color with paints or markers, make a pet rock!

Suncatchers

Materials: wax paper
             glitter
             food coloring
             popsicle sticks
             white glue

Give your child two sheets of wax paper. Set out dishes of food colouring mixed with white glue. Let kids use popsicle sticks to apply this mixture to the wax paper in swirling designs. Sprinkle glitter over glue. Cover with the second sheet of waxpaper and press lightly. Hang in the window!

GAMES

Slippery Slide

Materials: long piece of heavy-duty plastic
             hose
             grassy area

Lay the plastic on a grassy area and run water from a hose on the sheet to wet it. Leave the hose running at the top of the plastic. Children slide onto the sheet as far as possible.

Marble Croquet

Materials: pipe cleaners
             marbles
             tape

Set up a croquet course using pipe cleaners taped to the floor. Shoot the marbles through the pipe cleaners.

Bingo

(4 or more)
Everyone sits in a circle.
A ball is passed around the circle
while everyone sings:

    I knew a farmer who had a dog
    And Bingo was his name "O"
    B-I-N-G-O, B-I-N-G-O, B-I-N-G-O
    And Bingo was his name
The one who has the ball when the song ends is out.
Keep playing until no one is left.

Making Tents

Materials: deck of cards

Child takes two cards and tries to get them to stand upright by leaning them on each other. Try to make as many as possible.

Duck, Duck, Goose

(6 or more)

The player who is "it" is the goose. The other players are ducks. They sit in a circle. To start the game, the Goose walks around the outside of the circle, touching each player on the head. Each time Goose touches a player, Goose says "Duck." When Goose says "Goose," that player jumps up and runs the opposite direction around the circle. The first one back to the empty spot gets to sit down. The other person becomes the Goose.

Tiddlywinks

(1 or more)

Materials: tin can or bowl
          buttons

Each player gets four buttons plus a larger button to use as a flipper. Try to flip the pieces into the can. If you miss the can, you must flip the piece from where it lands. If playing with more than one, the first person to flip all his pieces into the can wins.

RECIPES

Peanut Butter Picnic Surprise

Banana
Peanut Butter
Bread

Remove the crust from the bread. Spread peanut butter on the bread. Roll the bread around the banana. Cut into tiny slices. (see photograph)

Fruit Fix Ups for Tots

Make baskets by cutting oranges in half, scooping out orange. Mix orange with other fruits if desired. Return to cleaned out orange peel. Cut a little peel around the top and make handle.

Corn Dogs

1	egg	1
1 cup	milk	250 ml
1/2 cup	cornmeal	125 ml
1/2 tsp.	salt	2 ml
1 tsp.	baking powder	5 ml
12	wieners	12
2 slices	cheddar cheese cut into 12 strips	2
	vegetable oil	

Mix first 5 ingredients in shallow bowl to make batter. Split wieners and insert a strip of cheese. Dip wiener into cornmeal batter and drop into hot oil, 375° (190°). Cook until golden brown. Drain on paper towels. Insert skewer in corn dog and serve with mustard and ketchup. Makes 12.

Camp Treats

2	graham crackers	2
2 sqs.	milk chocolate	2
	(or shavings of semi-sweet chocolate)	
1	marshmallow	1
	banana	
	tin foil	

On a sheet of tin foil, lay a graham cracker. On top of this lay a marshmallow sliced or pulled in half, a slice of banana and the chocolate. Place the second graham cracker on top, wrap up the sandwich in foil, and warm in the oven until gooey (180°C or 350°F oven for 5 minutes) or heat on the barbecue.

Banana Boats

peeled banana
mini marshmallows
chocolate chips
tin foil

Slice an opening lengthwise in the banana. Fill the opening with marshmallows and chocolate chips. Wrap in tin foil. Warm in the oven until gooey (180°C or 350°F for 5 minutes) Great for the barbecue too!

Fruit Popsicles

2 cups	sweetened pureed fruit (baby food)	500 ml
1 cup	orange juice	250 ml
1 tsp	sugar (optional)	5 ml

Mix and stir well. Freeze until hard.

Thumbprint Pies

1 cup	flour	250 ml
1 tsp.	salt	5 ml
1/3 cup plus 1 tbsp.	shortening	80 ml
2 tbsp.	water	30 ml

Mix all ingredients together. Roll dough into small balls. Mash each little ball down with your thumb so that it leaves a thumbprint. Bake at 350° for about 10 minutes. Remove from oven and let cool. Put jam, jelly, or peanut butter in the thumbprint. Sprinkle with powdered sugar. Can also use your favourite pie dough recipe.

BOOKS

Bourne, Miriam Ann. *Emilio's Summer Day*
Cook, Bernadine. *The Little Fish That Got Away*
De Regniers, Beatrice. *Who Likes The Sun!*
Lenski, Lois. *On a Summer's Day*
Low, Alice. *Summer*
Udry, Janice. *A Tree Is Nice*

Helpful Hint: Children learn by your example. If you are interested in reading - your child will most likely be interested in reading as well.

Fall Fantasies

FINGERPLAYS AND SONGS

Apple Fingerplay

I saw an apple red and round *(make apple shape with both hands)*
Lying down on the ground *(point)*
I cut it in half
And what did I see *(point to eye)*
A tiny star shining up at me *(cross hands across chest)*

1. *Cut an apple in half and show your child the star in the middle. Count the seeds in the center!*
2. *Do all apples have seeds? Why?*
3. *How many ways can you cut an apple? (lengthwise, sideways, halves, quarters.)*

Leaves

A little elf sat in a tree *(arch arms above head to make tree shape)*
Painting leaves to throw at me *(pretend to paint)*
Leaves of yellow, leaves of red
Came tumbling down upon my head *(flutter fingers from above heads down to floor)*

Apples

Way up high in the apple tree
(raise arms high above head, index fingers and thumbs make a circle)
Two little apples smiled at me
I shook that tree as hard as I could *(shake arms)*
And down came the apples*(drop one arm to knee, then drop other)*
M . . . m . . . m . . . were they good

Sneezing

Air comes in tickly
Through my nose *(breathe in)*
Then very quickly
Out it goes *(breathe out)*
Ahhh . . . Choo! *(sneeze)*
With every sneeze
I have to do
I make a breeze *(blow)*
Ahhh . . . Choo ! Ahhh . . . Choo! *(sneeze)*

Falling Leaves

The leaves are dropping from the trees
(flutter fingers up in air and to ground)
Yellow, brown and red
They patter softly like the rain *(tap fingers on floor)*
One landed on my head *(tap head)*

Apples, Apples

Apples, apples, in the tree *(point up high)*
One for you *(point to other person)*
And one for me *(point to self)*

Two Little Blackbirds

Two little blackbirds sitting on a hill *(hold up pointer fingers)*
One named Jack *(raise one pointer)*
One named Jill *(raise other pointer)*
Fly away Jack *(put pointer behind back)*
Fly away Jill *(put pointer behind back)*
Come back Jack *(bring pointer back)*
Come back Jill *(bring pointer back)*
May substitute children's names for Jack and Jill

Ten Little Leaves

(tune: 10 Little Indians)
1 little, 2 little, 3 little leaves
4 little, 5 little, 6 little leaves
7 little, 8 little, 9 little leaves
Blow them all away – whoof!

Two Little Houses

Two little houses all closed up tight *(make fist)*
Open up the windows and let in the light *(open fists)*
10 little finger people tall and straight *(10 fingers)*
Ready for breakfast at half past eight *(walk with fingers)*

Tony Chestnut

(tune: London Bridge)
Tony Chestnut knows I love you
*(touch toes, knees, chest, head, nose
in that order. At "I" point to self,
"loves" cross hands on chest, "you"
point to other person)*
Tony knows, Tony knows
(touch toes, knees, nose - repeat)
Tony Chestnut knows I love you
(actions same as line one)
That's what Tony knows
(one hand forward, other hand forward, touch toes, knees and nose)

ARTS AND CRAFTS

Fall Fingerpainting

Materials: crayons
           white paper (large)
           fingerpaint

After a talk about the colors of leaves, use colored crayons to color a large white sheet of paper (you will need to help). Then fingerpaint over the crayon. Interesting results!

Sponge Painting

Materials: old sponge (cut to approximately 1-2 inch squares)
           tempera paint
           paper (cut in shape of leaf)

Have child dip sponge into tempera paint and press onto leaf shape until leaf is colored.

Creative Collage

Materials: 1 cup from an egg carton
           white glue
           toothpick or Q-tip
           colored construction paper
           seeds

In egg cup put some white bondfast glue. On colored construction paper, your child can create his picture (he "paints" using the Q-tip or toothpick) dipped in glue. Then drop seeds on to make attractive artwork. You could use colored rice, macaroni, glitter, etc.

Leaf Rubbings

Materials: leaves
paper
crayons

Place leaf between two pieces of white paper. Have child color over leaf with flat sides of crayon. The leaf will come through in any color you choose. *You'll probably have to hold the paper while your child does the rubbings.

Paper Collage

Materials: brown construction paper
blue (optional) construction paper
colorful magazine
glue
scissors

After a walk and observing the trees in fall discuss the colors of leaves you saw. Cut out a tree trunk with many branches from brown construction paper. Glue onto sheet of blue construction paper (any color will do). Then have your child cut or tear small leaves to paste onto your tree. It will be colorful and beautiful.

Paper Plate Pictures

Materials: paper plate
collected items
glue

During a nature walk, collect fall things (or anything) your child thinks are pretty. When you get home paste these onto a sturdy paper plate. Your picture could collect coloured leaves, rocks, berries, twigs, etc. (Lepage's white glue will work)

Wax Gardens

Materials: flowers
colourful seeds
wax paper
iron
(optional) binding tape for framing picture.

1. Cut piece of wax paper double the size of the picture desired.
2. Let your child place flowers and/or seeds in an interesting design on a piece of wax paper.
3. One half of the paper is folded over top of the flowers, covering them.
4. Hold firmly and press with a warm iron. The wax paper will stick together and the flowers will show through in their bright colors.
5. The "picture" can then be framed with coloured tape. (optional)

Print Making

Materials: paper
thickly mixed tempera paint
fruit/vegetables cut in half

Press fruit or vegetables into the paint. Press design onto paper.

Leaf Prints

Materials: tempera paint
leaves
white paper
brush

Paint over leaf. Rub a clean white paper over. Pull off paper. Watch the thrill in your child's eye.

Apple Mobile

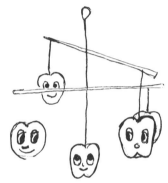

Materials: construction paper
scissors
crayons or felt pens, etc.

Draw an apple shape. Cut out and make a face on it. (child can do more depending on age) 4-5 apples strung and attached to a hanger would make a mobile.

Pressed Flower Pictures

Materials: flowers, leaves, etc.
thick paper (eg. bristol board)
clear mactac
yarn

Collect flowers and leaves from a nature walk and press them overnight. The next day have your child arrange the flattened flowers on a piece of heavy paper. Cover the arrangement with a circle of clear mactac. Attach a piece of yarn so the picture may be hung up.

Leaf People

Materials: paper (cut in leaf shapes)
paper scraps, buttons, cereal, etc.

Cut various leaf shapes for head, body, feet and arms. Glue on facial features, hair, buttons, etc. (*Could use the leaf rubbings you did from another day to cut out and make a person.)

Helpful Hint: Don't expect the pictures to look like you did them. Encourage your child and accept **anything** he does.

GAMES

Huntsman

(3 players or more)

"Huntsman" says to other players "Come with me to hunt bears." All players fall in line behind him and he marches along wherever he chooses while others follow. When huntsman has them far away from the home line he yells "bang." All players run home and the huntsman tries to catch as many as he can. The Huntsman then chooses a new Huntsman from players who were not caught.

*Younger children will need help.

Did You Ever See A Lassie?

(5 players or more)

Players join hands and walk in a circle while singing first two lines of song. *It* stands in center. On third line of song ("Go this way and that way") *It* does a movement and other players imitate him. *It* chooses a new *It* and game is played again.

Open The Gates As High As The Sky

(5 players or more)

1. Form a line while two children make a gate by facing each other, joining hands and raising arms high.
2. The "gate" says, "Open the gates as high as the sky, everyone come walking by."
3. Play music while the line of children walk through the gate.
4. When the music stops the "gate" catches one child.
5. The child who is caught chooses a partner to become the new gate. Children may be asked to walk, run, gallop, hop, skip, etc.

Helpful Hint: Buy a white tablecloth and some fabric crayons. Once a year have your child draw a picture (or as they get older they may want to write a message) on a piece of paper and iron onto a white tablecloth. What a precious keepsake that tablecloth will be one day for you and your child. (use for t-shirts, aprons, etc.).

RECIPES

Apple Sauce

apples

sugar

cinnamon (optional)

Wash, quarter, core and pare the apples; put into a saucepan. Add water to the depth of 2-3 cm. (1 inch). Cover pan and simmer until apples are soft. Add sugar to taste, allowing for each apple 15-30 ml (1-2 tbsp.) Stir until sugar is dissolved.

Apple Crisp

8 cups	sliced apples (medium, peeled)	2 l
3/4 cup	brown sugar packed	185 ml
1/2 cup	flour	125 ml
1/2 cup	oatmeal	125 ml
3/4 tsp.	cinnamon	4 ml
3/4 tsp.	nutmeg	4 ml
1/3 cup	butter	85 ml
1/2 cup	chopped nuts (optional)	125 ml

Preheat oven 375°F (190°C) Grease pan (8" x 8"). Place apple slices in pan. Mix remaining ingredients. Sprinkle over apples. Bake 30 minutes or until top is brown. Serve with cream or ice cream.

Apple Sherbet

6	apples	6
	(peeled, cored and quartered)	
1 cup	sugar	250 ml
1/2 cup	water	125 ml
1/3 cup	apple juice	85 ml

Combine sugar and water in a medium saucepan. Stir over medium heat until sugar is dissolved. Place apples in blender. Pour in sugar syrup and apple juice. Process until smooth. Pour into metal bowl. Cover and freeze until a 2" (5 cm) frozen border has formed around the edge (1-2 hours). Remove from freezer and beat until smooth. Return to freezer and freeze until sherbet is firm but not hard.

Helpful Hint: Be there for your child. They love your participation. If they choose to do it alone, be there to encourage and praise them.

Fresh Apples

Fresh apples are cored and divided into eighths. Serve with biscuits and cheese or yogurt. Add a shaker of cinnamon sugar, a dish of mixed nuts and peanut butter. Makes an easy and delicious dessert.

Baked Apples

apples
brown sugar
cinnamon
butter
marshmallows (optional)

Wash large apples and core. Cut a strip of peel from top of the apple. Place apples in a baking dish. Fill centers with brown sugar, a sprinkle of cinnamon and a bit of butter. Spoon brown sugar around apple (about 2 tbsp. per apple) Pour water into a dish to the depth of 1 inch (2 cm). Bake, basting several times until tender (30-40 min) at 350°F. (180°C) Test for tenderness with a paring knife in the center of the apple. Serve hot or cold with the syrup from the pan and/or with cream. (see photograph)

Optional: You can soften a marshmallow on each apple before removing from the pan.

BOOKS

Allington, Richard. *Autumn*
Barklem, Jill. *Autumn Story*
Fregosi, Claudia. *The Happy Horse*
Griffith, Helen V. *Alex Remembers*
Hopkins, Lee Bennett. *Merrily Comes Our Harvest In*
Kessler, Ethel & Leonard. *All For Fall*
Kumin, Maxine. *Follow the Fall*
Lapp, Eleanor. *The Mice Came In Early This Year*
Lenski, Eleanor. *Now It's Fall*
Taylor, Mark. *Henry Explores The Mountains*
Tresseh, Alvin R. *Autumn Harvest Johnny Maple Leaf*
Udry, Janice May. *Emily's Autumn*
Weygant, Naimi. *It's Autumn*
Zolotow, Charolette. *Say It!*

T hanksgiving
hrills

FINGERPLAYS AND SONGS

Mr. Turkey

Mr. Turkey is so tall and proud *(straighten self up tall)*
He dances on his feet *(make fingers dance in the air)*
And on each Thanksgiving Day *(hands in prayer)*
He's something good to eat *(pat your stomach)*

My Turkey

My turkey is so big and fat *(big circle with hands)*
He waddles when he walks *(hands on hips while walking slowly)*
His tail spreads out like a fan *(spread fingers of hands)*
He gobbles when he talks
He comes whenever he's hungry *(sprinkle imaginary grain seeds)*
But on Thanksgiving Day
Mr. Turkey if you're smart *(shake finger)*
You'll try to run away *(run on spot)*

"Gobble, Gobble, Gobble"

I heard Mr. Turkey say *(cup hand over ear)*
Gobble, gobble, gobble *(nod head)*
Soon it'll be Thanksgiving Day
Gobble, gobble, gobble *(nod head)*

People say that it is fun
But I think I shall run *(pretend to run)*
And hide until the day is done *(cover eyes)*
Gobble, gobble, gobble *(nod head)*
(For younger children do one verse only)

63

Five Little Pilgrims

On Thanksgiving Day
The first one says
"I'll have cake if I may" *(hold up one finger)*
The second one says
"I'll have turkey roasted" *(hold up two fingers)*
The third one says
"I'll have chestnuts toasted" *(hold up three fingers)*
The fourth one says
"I'll have pumpkin pie" *(hold up four fingers)*
The fifth one says
"My oh my!" *(hold up five fingers)*

The Brave Little Indian

The brave little Indian went looking for a bear
He looked in the woods and everywhere
The brave little Indian found a big bear
He ran like a rabbit! Oh, what a scare!

Gobble, Gobble, Gobble

(tune: Ever See a Lassie)
Gobble, gobble, gobble, fat turkey, fat turkey
I'm not here for living
I'm here for Thanksgiving
Gobble, gobble, gobble, fat turkey am I

A Funny Bird

(tune: Yankee Doodle)
The turkey is a funny bird *(place hand above eyes)*
His head goes wobble, wobble *(turn from side to side)*
And all he says is just one word *(look surprised, hands in air)*
Gobble, gobble, gobble *(run in place)*

Turkey in the Barnyard

Turkey in the barnyard
What does he say?
Gobble, gobble, gobble all day
Turkey on the table
What do you say?
Yummy, yummy, yummy all day
Turkey in my tummy
What do you say?
I ate too much turkey
On Thanksgiving Day!

ARTS AND CRAFTS

Turkey Bag

Materials: paper grocery bag
            magazine
            stapler or glue
            scissors

Open a large grocery bag. Cut out eyes. In the inside fold, cut out arm holes so that your child can wear the bag. Decorate with magazine feathers. Have child tear the feathers from the magazine. (They don't have to be perfect)

Collage

Materials: seeds (pumpkin, sunflower, apple, etc.)
            paper
            glue
            pencil

Make designs (turkey, pilgrims' hat) on a piece of paper. The child could then paint the inside of the figure with white glue. The seeds can be arranged or placed at random on the glue.

Handsome Turkey

Materials: paper
            crayons

Trace child's hand on paper. Put feather lines in fingers. Draw line across the bottom. Draw legs, put beak, comb and eyes on.

Paper Bag Turkey

Materials: construction paper
            tempera paint
            paper bag (lunch size)
            newspaper
            string
            scissors
            glue

Stuff a brown paper bag with newspapers. Tie the end tight using string. The end can be shaped to make the turkey's head. Paint his body brown and his head red. Construction paper can be used to make his tail feathers and wattle.

Helpful Hint: Encourage your child to do as much by himself as he can. Don't do it for him.

Paper Plate Turkey

Materials: paper plate
paint
colored paper or magazine
glue
scissors

Paint paper plate brown. Draw and cut out feathers and glue to top half of paper plate. Make head and feet. Glue feet to bottom of the paper plate. Make an accordian neck from two pieces of long narrow paper. Glue turkey's head to the accordian neck. Add and paste to center of paper plate.

Playdough Beads

Materials: playdough
toothpick
tempera paint
yarn or twine

Shape playdough into small balls. Push a toothpick through for stringing later with heavy yarn or twine. Paint when dry. String with yarn.

Thanksgiving Place Mat

(A treasured keepsake)
Materials: construction paper
glue
leaves
mactac

Have child collect leaves on an outdoor walk. Glue the leaves in any fashion onto the paper. Ask the child what he is thankful for and write "I am thankful for . . . " on the paper. Put the childs name on it. Cover with mactac. Your child can use his placemat at mealtime, or give it as a gift to someone special. Optional: Use pinking shears to cut edges.

Tee Pees

Materials: newspaper
string

Fanfold a newspaper. Make into the shape of a teepee. Tie a string around the top. (1/4 of the way down.)

Indian Necklace

Materials: tempera paint and brush
macaroni   string

Paint macaroni and then string to make an Indian necklace.

Indian Headband

Materials: construction paper
        scissors
        glue or tape
        crayons or markers

Cut out colored feathers from construction paper. Have your child decorate using crayons or markers. Cut a one inch wide strip of dark colored construction paper long enough so it will fit snug over your child's head when glued together. Then glue the feathers onto the band.

Variation: Cut the band first and have your child make designs on head band with seeds. (corn, sunflower, peas, beans, etc.)

Horn of Plenty

Materials: brown construction paper
        magazines
        scissors
        glue

Draw a horn of plenty using brown construction paper. Have your child flip through magazines to find all the food he likes. Cut them out and paste them on the horn of plenty.

Balloon Turkey

Materials: balloon
        construction paper
        magazine
        glue
        scissors

Blow up a round balloon and tie the end. Cut out turkey tail feathers from brightly colored magazine pictures, paste on balloon. Add head, feet, beak and eyes from construction paper. A colourful project!

GAMES

Follow the String

Materials: a Thanksgiving favor for each child
        string

Hide party favors all over the room. Attach strings to each favor and wind the string around various pieces of furniture. Each child is given the end of the string and they begin to follow the strings until the favors are found. Please don't wind the strings around breakable objects. Ideas for favors: Thanksgiving Day stickers, your child's favourite fruit, etc.

Turkey Gobbler Game

1. The turkeys line up in a row against one end of play area.
2. The farmer stands in the middle of the room and calls out
   "Turkey gobblers in the street
   If I catch you – you I'll eat"
3. On the word "eat" all the turkeys must run to the other side of the play area.
4. Those caught become the farmer's helpers and can also call out the verse.
5. The last turkey caught becomes the next farmer.

Turkey Chase

Gobble, Gobble, said the turkey *(nod your head)*
Soon it'll be Thanksgiving Day *(shake your finger)*
How are you going to treat me? *(point to self)*
Are you going to eat me? *(pretend to eat)*
Then I will run away *(child runs away and hides and parent tries to catch)*

Variation: Use as fingerplay and have child use fingers to show running away.

Corn Hunt

Materials: kernels of corn
Hide as many kernels of corn as desired around the room. When the game starts the child tries to find the corn in a given length of time. At the end of time limit each child can count how many kernels each has, then each child should be rewarded for doing so well.

Where is the Turkey?

Materials: picture or small toy turkey
Child leaves the room. While the child is gone the turkey is hidden. When the child comes back, guide him to the turkey's whereabouts by playing "hot" or "cold". As the child gets closer to the turkey, he becomes "hotter" and "hotter". If he turns away from the turkey, he becomes "cold".

RECIPES

Autumn Soup

(2 servings)

1/2 lb.	stewing beef (cubed)	250 g
1/2 cup	chopped onions	125 ml
2/3 cup	diced celery	165 ml
2 cups	water	500 ml
2/3 cup	diced potatoes	165 ml
1 tsp	salt	5 ml
1/4 tsp.	pepper	1 ml
1	bay leaf, crumbled	1
1/2 tsp.	basil	2 ml
3	whole tomatoes, fresh	3

Brown beef in stew pot. Add onions and celery. Fry until soft. Add water, salt, pepper, bay leaf, basil, tomatoes and potatoes. Simmer until meat is cooked.

Apple Snow

1 cup	grated apple	250 ml
3/4 cup	icing sugar	185 ml
2	egg whites	2

Place all ingredients in mixing bowl and beat with electric mixer until stiff enough to form firm peaks. May be served with jello or plain with whipped cream topping.

Nut Balls

1 cup	chocolate chips	250 ml
1/2 lb.	peanuts	

Melt chocolate chips over low heat. Take pan off the stove and add peanuts. Stir well and drop by spoonfuls onto waxed paper. Chill in refrigerator.

Frozen Fruit Salad

3 oz.	cream cheese	84 g
1 cup	mayonnaise	250 ml
4 oz.	crushed pineapple	112 g
2 tbsp.	pineapple juice	30 ml
1-1/2 cup	small marshmallows (halved)	375 ml
1 cup	whipping cream	250 ml

Mix mayonnaise and cream cheese. Add pineapple juice and marshmallows. Stir together. Whip cream until it stands in white mountains. Mix whipped cream into marshmallow mixture. Pour into mould. Freeze. (serves 8)

Cornstacks

2 - 6 oz. pkgs.	butterscotch bits
1 can	chow mein noodles
1 can	peanuts

Melt butterscotch bits in a pan. Stir in peanuts and chow mein noodles. Drop by teaspoons onto wax paper.

Coconut Crackers

	graham crackers	
1 tsp.	brown sugar	5 ml
1/2 tsp	butter	2 ml
	coconut	

Place graham crackers in pan. Sprinkle 1 tsp. of brown sugar on each. Put 1/2 tsp. butter on the sugar. Put one tbsp. coconut on top of the butter. Put under the broiler until coconut is browned and the butter melted.

Hot Apple Cider

2 - 48 oz. tins	apple juice	3 litres
1 cup	brown sugar	250 ml
2 - 2"	cinnamon sticks	50mm
12	whole cloves	12
1 tsp.	whole allspice	5 ml

Put spices in a little bag.
Simmer until hot and spicy.

BOOKS

Akott, Louisa. *An Old Fashioned Thanksgiving*
Balian, Lorna. *Sometimes It's Turkey, Sometimes It's Feathers*
Dalgliesh, Alice. *The Thanksgiving Story*
Devlin, Wende. *Cranberry Thanksgiving*
Glovach, Linda. *The Little Witch's Thanksgiving Book*
Janice. *Little Bear's Thanksgiving*
Ott, John. *Peter Pumpkin*
Schulz, Charles. *Charlie Brown Thanksgiving*
Tresseh, Alvin. *Autumn Harvest*
Williams, Barbara. *Chester Chipmunk's Thanksgiving*

Halloween **owls**

FINGERPLAYS AND SONGS

A Haunted House
(tune: Are You Sleeping)
1. Tiptoe, tiptoe, tiptoe, tiptoe
   Knock on the door, knock on the door
   Here comes Jack-O-Lantern
   Here comes Jack-O-Lantern
   Run, run, run, run, run, run!
2. Funny goblins
3. Scary ghosts

Ghostie
(whisper) See my big and scary eyes *(use thumb and index finger to make glasses for eyes)*
Look out now, a big surprise
(shout) Boo! *(remove fingers from eyes)*

Halloween Witch
Here's a witch with a tall, tall, hat
(make triangle shape with hands above head)
Two green eyes on a black, black cat
(point to eyes)
Jack-O-Lantern in a row
(pretend to march)
And goblins laughing ho, ho, ho!
(hold tummy and laugh)

Witches

(tune: One Little, Two Little, Three Little Indians)
One little, two little, three little witches,
Fly over haystacks, fly over ditches
Slide down the moon without any hitches
Hey, ho, Halloween's here

I'm A Little Pumpkin

(tune: I'm A Little Teapot)
I'm a little pumpkin, short and stout
Packed full of seeds, that you can take out
When you are all finished
Then I'll be
The very best jack-o-lantern, you have ever seen

Three Black Cats

(tune: Three Blind Mice)
Three black cats, three black cats
Sit on the fence, sit on the fence
They've all been into some witches brew
They tease all the dogs and the neighbours, too
Did you ever see such a hallabaloo?
On Halloween!

Three Little Witches

One little, two little, three little witches *(put appropriate fingers up)*
Ride through the sky on a broom *(run in a circle)*
One little, two little, three little witches
Wink their eyes at the moon *(blink eyes)*

Coal Black Cat

Coal black cat with hump on back *(hold tight fist downward)*
Shining eyes so yellow *(hold hands in circles around eyes)*
See him with his funny tail *(one finger through fist and wiggle it)*
He's a funny fellow

Halloween Ghost

I sway in the breeze *(sway from left to right)*
I fly through the trees *(flap arms in flying motion)*
I'm a Halloween ghost *(point to yourself)*
Boo! Boo! – Boo! Boo! *(put one hand on each side of
the mouth, megaphone fashion, as if to magnify the
sound. Face left on first Boo! Boo! And then right on
the second Boo! Boo!*

Halloween Will Soon Be Here

(tune: London Bridge)

1. Halloween will soon be here
   Soon be here (2)
   Halloween will soon be here
   Look out children
2. Witches riding on a broom
3. Black cats howling on a fence
4. Goblins hiding in the dark
5. Strange things happening all around

ARTS AND CRAFTS

Yarn Ghosts

Materials: glue
white yarn or string
black construction paper
ring binder reinforcement

Glue white yarn on black construction paper or newspaper. Use ring binder reinforcements for eyes. (see photograph)

Marshmallow Ghosts

Materials: marshmallows
kleenex or napkin
elastic
felt pens

Use marshmallows for head, cover with kleenex and secure with elastic. Draw on features with a marker. (see photograph)

Playdough Pumpkins

Materials: orange playdough
cloves or seeds

Make pumpkins from orange playdough.
Add cloves or seeds for features.
(see photograph)

Helpful Hint: Guide your child to look upon Halloween as an opportunity to let their imaginations soar and share their fun and excitement and treats with others.

Halloween Bag Puppets

Materials: paper bag
construction paper
pipe cleaners

Paint bag first if desired and paste on shapes for features. Use pipe cleaners for whiskers. (see photograph)

orange pumpkin   black cat   brown owl

Witch With Scraggly Hair

Materials: newspaper
construction paper
felt pens

Use newspaper strips for hair, pre-cut black witch's hat and give child jiffy marker to draw features. (see photograph)

Flying Ghosts

Materials: construction paper
crayons
thread

Draw ghost shapes on white construction paper. Use crayons to decorate the ghosts. Cut strips of construction paper for hair and glue them to the ghosts. Hang them from the ceiling on a thread.

Paper Bag Pumpkins

Materials: paper bag
newspaper
masking tape
paint

Stuff a paper bag with crushed newspaper. Twist the remainder of the bag into a thick stem. Wrap masking tape around the stem so it is secure. Paint the pumpkin. Then paste or paint festive features on the pumpkin. (see photograph)

Shadow Box

Materials: flashlight   paper bag
crepe paper or tissue paper

Cut away features on the base of a bag and line it with black or orange crepe or tissue paper. Insert a flashlight and twist the rest of the bag around the handle, leaving an opening for the switch. Children love to turn on the flashlight when the room is dark.

Helpful Hint: Children can dance to music. For example, flying, dancing, gliding, scaring, prowling, riding broomsticks, slinking, etc.

Skeletons

Materials: white drinking straws or toothpicks
glue
scissors
black construction paper
white paper

The drinking straws should be cut in a variety of lengths. Have your child glue the straw bits to black construction paper. The skeleton's skull can be cut from white paper. (see photograph)

Masks on a Stick

Materials: coat hanger
old nylon
scraps of felt
cloth and yarn
glue

Precover wire with old nylon for child. (Show him how you did it.) Your child can make the faces on the mask by gluing on scraps of felt, cloth and yarn. (see photograph)

Halloween Bag

Materials: paper bag
scraps
glue
scissors

Prefold a cuff around a large paper bag. Staple or glue on a handle. Have child decorate his own bag. Have him cut or tear Halloween shapes. (see photograph)

Folded Paper Owls

fold back   fold front   add paper eyes,
beak and claws

Helpful Hint: Show children funny, spooky, scary, sad, happy, exciting, creepy, frightening and mysterious through facial expressions and body movement.

Helpful Hint: Use the basic shapes to make witches, goblins, and cats. Have precut circles, triangles, squares, and rectangles in black and green. Let the children use their own imaginations when making their Halloween figures.

GAMES

Games For A Halloween Party

1. Act out the character you are.
2. Hide numbers from 1-10 (or however many are at the party) inside blown up balloons. Have little gifts with duplicate numbers. The child picks the gift the same as the number in the balloon.
3. Toss balls into Jack-O-Lantern treat holders.
4. Hide paper Jack-O-Lanterns around the room for children to find. Have an individual or team winner.
5. Guess how many peanuts there are in the jar.
6. Play pin the tail on the black cat.
7. Broomstick Relay
   Divide children in teams of equal numbers and line them up at one end of the room. The first player on each team rides a broom to the goal line and back to his place. The second player does the same. Let them run 2 to 3 times each so that each child gets to enjoy riding the broom a few times.
8. *Tune: Farmer in the Dell*
   Tonight is Halloween, tonight is Halloween
   It's a merry scary night
   Tonight is Halloween
   The child picks a pumpkin, the child picks a pumpkin,
   On this merry scary night, the child picks a pumpkin
   The pumpkin picks an owl . . .
   The owl picks a ghost . . . witch . . . goblin . . . cat . . . bat . . .
   The bat flies away . . .
   Whoever catches the bat first becomes the child to start a new game.

RECIPES

Witches Brew

2 large tins unsweetened orange juice
2 large tins cranberry juice
2 large tins gingerale
Mix in punch bowl. Sneak in a piece of dry ice.
Chant: "Andy, dandy, fiddle-few
           Happy, yappy witches brew"

Helpful Hint: Dramatize buying a pumpkin at the store, dressing up in different costumes and giving out treats at your house.

Sugar Cookies

Use your favourite recipe. Children can frost with icing and add features with chocolate chips.

Note: Tupperware has a jack-o-lantern cutter.

Halloween Snack

Cut circle shapes out of bread slices and spread cheez whiz over bread and make jack-o-lantern face with raisins. Serve with witches broomsticks. (carrot sticks)

Caramel Apples

	wax paper	
16	small apples	16
4 cups	melted caramels	1 litre
2 tbsp.	butter	30 ml
3 tsp.	vanilla	15 ml
16	popsicle sticks	16

Melt butter and caramels. Add vanilla. Push popsicle stick into apple and swirl into caramel mixture. Place onto waxed paper to cool.

Pumpkin Cake

2 cups	pumpkin	500 ml
1 cup	oil	250 ml
1/3 cup	water	65 ml
3-1/2 cups	flour	875 ml
3 cups	sugar	750 ml
4	eggs	4
1 cup	nuts	250 ml
2 tsp.	cinnamon	10 ml
1 tsp.	cloves, nutmeg, ginger (1/3 of each)	5 ml
1-1/2 tsp.	vanilla	7 ml
1-1/2 tsp.	soda	7 ml
2 tsp.	baking powder	10 ml

Make a jack-o-lantern. Clean the inside of the pumpkin saving the seeds for spring planting and tasting. Your child can help make a cake from above recipe. Pour the cake in a large round pan and bake at 350° for 35 min. Ice the cake with orange icing and put a face on with colored candy.

Helpful Hint: Draw a pumpkin on the 31st day of the calendar so your child can see when Halloween will be. Each day you can count with your child how many days until the 31st.

Carve A Pumpkin

- Carve out the pumpkin. Feel and smell the pulp. Cook the pulp. Make muffins or pie.
- Scoop out the seeds. Place them on a cookie sheet. Sprinkle with salt. Bake until they turn a light brown.
- Save a seed before baking, plant it in the spring.

Jack-O-Lantern

Put a scoop of orange sherbert on a plate. Stick a candle in the top and add chocolate chips or gumdrops for the eyes, nose, and mouth.

BOOKS

Balian, Lorna. *The Humbug Witch*
Bright, Robert. *Georgie's Halloween*
Calhoun, Mary. *Wobble the Witch Cat*
Delage, Ida. *What Does A Witch Need?*
Foster, Doris. *Tell Me Mr. Owl*
Freeman, Don. *Space Witch, Tilly Witch*
Keats, Ezra Jack. *Hi Cat!*
Miles, Betty. *A Day of Autumn*
Owens, Judy. *Halloween Fun*
Ross, Geraldine. *Scat the Witches Cat*
Slobodkin, Louis. *Trick or Treat*
Stevens, Carla. *Rabbit and Skunk and Spooks*
Unwin, Nora. *Proud Pumpkin*
Yezback, Steven. *Pumpkin Seeds*
Zion, Gene. *The Meanest Squirrel I Ever Met*

Q. Why did the witches go on strike?
A. They wanted electric brooms.

Q. Where do bats get their energy?
A. From their bat-trees.

Q. Where did the little bat have to go?
A. To the bat-room.

Helpful Hint: When borrowing books from the library, take them out at least one month in advance, in order to avoid disappointment.

Helpful Hint: Because your child is too small to carve the pumpkin, have him draw the eyes, nose and mouth with a jiffy marker. You can carve it out with a knife.

C hristmas reations

FINGERPLAYS AND SONGS

Ho! Ho! Ho!

Here is Santa big and fat *(show Santa big and fat)*
A hat upon his curly head *(peak hand sat top of head)*
He will see me Christmas night *(hold hands in circles around eyes)*
When I'm fast asleep in bed *(rest head in hands)*
Ho! Ho! Ho! O deary me
I must be as good as I can be *(point finger)*

I Am A Christmas Tree

I am a Christmas tree
(make a triangle shape with hands above head)
As straight and tall as I can be
(stand straight and tall)
At the very top is a shiny light
(point up)
Each little candle twinkles bright
(hold up both hands - wiggle fingers)

Santa

Two merry blue eyes, a funny little nose
(point to eyes, point to nose)
A long, snowy beard and cheeks like a rose
(pull at chin and pinch cheeks)
A round chubby form *(pat tummy)*
A big, bulging pack *(pat back)*
Hurrah! for old Santa! *(jump up and down, hands in air)*
We're glad he's come back

Here is the Chimney

Here is the chimney *(make fist)*
Here is the top *(place flat hand over fist)*
Take off the lid *(remove flat hand)*
Out Santa will pop *(put thumb up)*

Here Is Old Santa

Here is old Santa *(hold up right thumb)*
Here is his sleigh *(hold up left thumb)*
Here are the reindeer
Which he drives away *(hold up eight fingers)*
Dasher, Dancer, Prancer, Vixen,
Comet, Cupid, Donner, Blitzen *(one finger down as each name is called)*
Away they go! *(put thumbs together and soar off into the air)*

Santa

(tune: Merrily We Roll Along)
Santa's funny and he's fat
He is jolly and he's kind
And he visits every home
With children on his mind

Elves

The elves worked with one hammer, one hammer, one hammer *(pretend your hammering with one hand)*
The elves worked with two hammers, two hammers, two hammers *(pretend your hammering using both hands)*
The elves work with three hammers, three hammers, three hammers *(hammer using both hands and one foot)*
The elves worked with four hammers, four hammers, four hammers *(hammer with both hands and both feet)*

The Christmas Tree

(tune: Here We Go Round The Mulberry Bush)
1. What do we put on the Christmas tree
   The Christmas tree, the Christmas tree
   What do we put on the Christmas tree
   The pretty Christmas tree
2. We put some bells on the Christmas tree
3. We put a star on the Christmas tree
4. We put some lights on the Christmas tree

Santa Claus

(tune: London Bridge)
1. Santa Claus is coming soon
   Coming soon, coming soon
   Santa Claus is coming soon
   Good old Santa
2. Santa wears a big red coat
3. Santa wears a big red hat
4. Santa wears big black boots
5. Santa wears big white mittens
6. Santa has a big white beard
7. Santa Claus is very fat
8. Santa Claus has eight reindeer

Christmas Song (or round)

(tune: Row, Row, Row Your Boat)
Sing, sing, sing be glad
Christmas time is here
For every girl and every boy
The best day of the year

ARTS AND CRAFTS

Life Size Santa

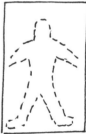

Materials: large piece of paper
    optional: use newspaper
    pencil
    paint and brush
    cotton batting
    glue

Have your child lay down on a large piece of paper and trace his body. When this is finished adjustments are made to make Santa more realistic.

These are the adjustments:
   1. make tummy nice and fat
   2. a cap is made for his head
   3. draw his belt and boots
   4. draw eyes, ears, nose and mouth.

The Santa can then be painted and cotton batting can be used for his beard. (see photograph)

Paper Plate Santa

Materials: paper plate
            cotton batting
            construction paper
            glue
            scissors

Use small paper plate for Santa's head. Use cotton batting beard, ball on tip of hat, eyebrows, trim on bottom of hat. Use construction paper for hat and facial features. (see photograph)

Miniature Ornaments

Materials: walnut shells (halved)
            Q-tip or toothpick
            glue
            glitter
            scissors
            tiny cutouts from Christmas cards

Child glues cutouts inside the walnut shells. Use a toothpick or Q-tip to paint a thin line of glue around the edge of the shells. Sprinkle glitter on.

Pipe-Cleaner Candy Cane

Materials: red and white pipe cleaner
Wind a red and white pipe cleaner together
 and bend at the top.
(see photograph)

Candle Holder

Materials: red construction paper
            popsicle sticks or straws
            toilet paper roll
            pine cones or other
            small Christmas decorations
            tempera paint
            brush

Make a circle about 5 inches in diameter out of red construction paper. Have your child cut it out. Paste sticks around the toilet paper roll. Paint. Glue the toilet paper roll to the center of the circle. Add pine cones, ribbon, etc. around base of toilet paper roll to give Christmasy effect. (see photograph)

Glitter Trees

Materials: white or colored baking cups
  glue
  glitter
  white paper

Paper baking cups are glued to a piece of heavy paper to form a tree shape. Frilly edges of the trees can be decorated by gluing on glitter. (see photograph)

Bell

Materials: 1 egg cup segment
  paint
  foil
  glitter
  glue
  bell
  string

Paint one egg cup segment and let it dry or cover it with foil. Place glue where you think it should be and cover with glitter. Tie a string to end of bell and pull the string through the top of the egg carton. (see photograph)

Christmas Ornaments

Materials: playdough
  cologne (optional)
  wax paper
  rolling pin
  cookie cutters
  glitter, sequins, etc.

Add food coloring to playdough. Also add a few drops of cologne. Roll dough on waxed paper. Cut out shapes with cookie cutters. Trim with glitter, etc. Remember to poke a hole at the top so that you can string your decoration. When shapes are dry, they may be hung on the Christmas tree.

Egg Carton Christmas Tree

Materials: egg carton
  glue
  stiff paper
  scissors
  tinsel

Cut apart the cups of an egg carton. Glue them on a piece of paper in the shape of a tree. Wind tinsel through it. (see photograph)

Santa Claus

Materials: construction paper
(red, white, black)
paper plate
cotton batting
glue

Make a white circle for face. Red triangle for hat, pie plate for the body, hands and belt are cut from red construction paper. Boots and buckle are cut from black construction paper. Use the cotton batting for beard and brows. Facial features can be coloured on. While you draw the shape your child can cut out the big shapes. Glue body parts together.

GAMES

Christmas Tree Game

(2 or more)
Draw a Christmas tree on a large paper. Each child, blindfolded draws a bell on the tree.

Follow Rudolf

(2 or more)
Rudolf wears a red circle construction paper nose and leads the group of reindeer. What he does everyone must do. (play like follow the leader.) Keep exchanging "Rudolf", so that all children can have a turn being the leader.

Santa On His Sleigh

(tune: Farmer In The Dell)
1. Santa's on his sleigh (2)
   Hi Ho, it's Christmas time
   Santa's on his sleigh
2. The elf picks a reindeer
3. The reindeer picks a toy
4. The toy picks a box
5. The box picks some wrap
6. The wrap picks a bow
7. The presents are all ready

(play as in "The Farmer In The Dell")

Freeze

Children march in time to the music. When music stops, children "freeze" or stand perfectly still.

Where's Rudolf?

(5 or more)
(It's Foggy Out and Santa Can't Find Rudolf)
Form a circle. Two children are in the circle, one blindfolded "Santa" and the other child is "Rudolf." Santa calls Rudolf and tries to touch him by listening for his voice. Rudolf answers and tries to avoid Santa's touch. When Santa touches Rudolf the child can remove the blindfold and two other children can become Santa and Rudolf.
*Keep children in circle so they don't get hurt.

Santa Follow the Leader

Play follow the leader in the snow. When new snow has fallen, an adult can go first and make footprints. Children follow the footprints.

Santa's Punching Bag

An old pillow case or laundry bag can be stuffed with rags. Tie or sew ends together. Children can release energy by punching, kicking and slapping the bag.

RECIPES

Plum Pudding

1 can of plums
white cake mix
Mix one can of plums with a box of white cake mix. (do not add water or eggs.) Bake for 25 minutes at 350°F.

Popcorn Xmas Trees

1-3/4 cup	icing sugar	435 ml
1	egg white, unbeaten	1
1/4 tsp.	vinegar	1 ml
8	icecream cones	8
6 cups	popped corn	1.5 l
	decorations	

Combine sugar, egg and vinegar and beat until icing is smooth; add sugar to spreading consistency. Cover cones with icing and roll in loose popcorn. When dry, decorate with bits of cherries, sugar coated almonds or cinnamon drops. Stick on with icing.

Stained Glass Cookies

1 cup	margarine	250 ml
1 cup	shortening	250 ml
1 cup	sugar	250 ml
1/4 cup	honey	60 ml
2	eggs	2
2 tsp.	vanilla	10 ml
5 cups	flour	1-1/4 litre
1 tsp.	baking soda	5 ml
1 tsp.	salt	5 ml

hard candies (lollipops, lifesavers)

Mix margarine, shortening, sugar, honey, eggs and vanilla. Add flour, soda, and salt. Chill dough overnight. On waxed paper roll out the dough and cut out shapes with cookie cutters. Then cut out areas for windows.

or

Roll dough into "snakes". Shape the snakes into cookies, leave open spaces. Place cookies on well greased cookie sheet. Fill openings with crushed hard cookies or whole life savers. Bake at 350° for 7-8 minutes. Let cookies cool for 5 minutes before removing from cookie sheet. Can be used as edible decorations on the tree. (see photograph)

Santa Claus Eggs

eggs (1/2 for each serving)
plus 1 for trimming
whole fresh tomato
whole cloves (2 for each 1/2 egg)
lettuce leaves

Hard boil as many eggs as you need. Cool 20 minutes. Peel eggs, cut eggs in half lengthwise and set them yolk up on wax paper. Remove yolk from extra egg and slice the white part into 1/4" sections. From these slices, cut halves of Santa's mustache. Also cut small triangles for the tip of each hat. To make Santa's hat, scoop out pulp and cut out a triangle from the skin. Cut an oval from the nose. Use a toothpick to attach hat to the egg. The yolk of the egg is Santa's face. Press in 2 cloves to form eyes. (Don't eat cloves.) Below them, place the nose and mustache.

CUT SLICES
← THEN
SHAPES →

Hat Tip

MUSTACHE

Gingerbread Men

5 cups	flour	1-1/4 litres
1/2 tsp.	salt	2 ml
3 tsp.	cinnamon	15 ml
2 tsp.	ginger	10 ml
1 tsp.	cloves	5 ml
1 tsp.	nutmeg	5 ml
1 cup	shortening	250 ml
1 cup	sugar	250 ml
1 cup	molasses	250 ml
2	eggs	2
	decorations (raisins, chocolate chips, icing, etc.)	

Mix flour, salt, cinnamon, ginger, cloves and nutmeg in a bowl. Beat shortening with sugar in large bowl until fluffy. Beat in molasses and eggs. Stir in flour mixture to make stiff dough. Chill one hour. Roll out about 1/4" thick and cut into gingerbread men. Decorate with whatever you choose, be creative, or decorate with icing after the gingerbread men are baked. Bake at 350F for 12-15 minutes.

Poppycock

1 cup	pecans halved	250 ml
2/3 cup	almonds	165 ml
1 cup	sunflower seeds	250 ml
1 cup	peanuts	250 ml
8 cups	popped corn	2 l
Syrup:		
1-1/3 cup	brown sugar	335 ml
1 cup	margarine	250 ml
1/2 cup	corn syrup	125 ml
1/2 tsp.	baking soda	2 ml
1 tsp.	vanilla	5 ml
1 tsp.	cream of tartar	5 ml

Cook syrup until hard ball stage (about 3 min.) Remove from heat and add baking soda, vanilla and cream of tartar. Add everything to syrup mixture except the popped corn and stir well. Pour mixture over popped corn and mix. Spread mixture onto cookie sheet to cool. Store in covered container.

Hard ball stage: Mixture forms a hard ball in cold water which will hold its shape when pressed.

BOOKS

Carley, Wayne. *Charley The Mouse Finds Christmas.*
Darling, Kathy. *The Mystery in Santa's Toyshop.*
de Brunhoff, Laurent. *Babar's Christmas Tree.*
De Lage, Ida. *ABC Christmas.*
Devlin, Wendy & Harry. *Cranberry Christmas.*
Fenner, Carol. *Christmas Tree on the Mountain.*
Hoff, Syd. *Where's Prancer?*
Hutchins, Pat. *The Silver Christmas Tree.*
Irion, Ruth Hershey. *The Christmas Tree Cookie.*
Kay, Helen. *A Stocking for a Kitten.*
Krol, Steven. *Santa's Crash-Bang Christmas.*
Lindgren, Astrid. *Christmas In Noisy Village.*
Low, Joseph. *The Christmas Grump.*
Wells, Rosemary. *Morris' Disappearing Bag*
Zakhader, Boris. *How A Piglet Crashed the Christmas Party.*

 Sleepytime activities

FINGERPLAYS AND SONGS

Sleep
To make my body strong I find
I need much sleep and rest of mind
Sh sh sh sh . . .
So into bed I climb at night
Without a fuss, turn out the light
Sh sh sh sh . . .

Bedtime
This little fellow is ready for bed *(extend index finger)*
Down on his pillow he lays his head *(lay finger in palm of other hand)*
Pulls up the covers, snug and tight *(close fingers over fellow in palm)*
And this is the way he sleeps all night *(close eyes)*

Wiggles
I wiggle my fingers *(wiggle fingers)*
I wiggle my toes *(wiggle toes)*
I wiggle my shoulders *(wiggle shoulders)*
I wiggle my nose *(wiggle nose)*
Now no more wiggles are left in me *(lay down in bed)*
So I will be still as still can be *(lay still)*

Helpful Hint: Make exercise a daily habit. Be sure your child exercises during the day to help his body tell his mind not to forget going to bed.

Time To Rest

It's time to rest, to rest your head *(put right forefinger in left palm)*
Snuggle down in your own little bed *(rock finger back and forth)*
Covered up tight in blankets so warm *(cover with left fingers)*
Safe and cozy and away from all harm *(bring hands to cheek, bend head against hands, close eyes)*

Soft Steps

(tune: Are You Sleeping)
Tippy tippy tiptoe
Tippy tippy tiptoe
Let us go (2)
Tippy tippy tiptoe (2)
To and fro (2)

Tippy tippy tiptoe (2)
Through the house (2)
Tippy tippy tiptoe (2)
Soft as a mouse (2)

Here is the Church

Here is the church *(interlock fingers together with fingers inside hands)*
Here is the steeple *(bring out pointer fingers to make steeple shape)*
Open the doors *(pull thumbs apart)*
And see all the people *(open hands so that fingers are exposed being the people in the church)*

Sleeping, Sleeping Little Star

(tune: Twinkle, Twinkle, Little Star)
Sleeping sleeping little star
Stretching as you shine so far
Stretching out your shining light
Shining in the sky so bright
Sleeping sleeping little star
Stretching as you shine so far

Sleepy Time

Ten chubby fingers, ten little toes *(point to suggested body parts)*
Two shiny eyes, one little nose
Two listening ears, one nodding head
Shut sleepy eyes, go off to bed *(shut eyes)*

Baby, Baby In Your Bed

(tune: Twinkle Twinkle Little Star)
Baby, baby, in your bed
You cannot lift your tired head
But you can reach your arms way out
Reach and stretch them all about
Reach your arms way up so high
Reach and stretch them to the sky

Baby, baby in your bed
You cannot lift your tired head
But you can reach your legs way out
Reach and stretch them all about
Reach your legs way up so high
Reach and stretch them to the sky

Hints to help relax before bedtime

- Listen to quiet tapes or records.
- Listen to a story and tape.
- Wiggling body parts - child wiggles and stops when you tell him to. The activity helps relieve any tension.
- Play a quiet game of cards.
- Play a quiet board game.
- Tell an eyes-closed story. Children love to hear of when you were little or make-up a story. When the lights are out tell your story very slowly and in a quiet voice (almost a whisper) just loud enough for your child to hear.
- Child may look at books.
- Play "I spy": Say "I spy with my little eye something that is (name a color.)" Child tries to find the object you are looking at. When he does find the object, then it's the child's turn to "spy" a color of an object. Choose objects that are very obvious!
- Read a book to your child.
- Always follow a routine so that your child becomes used to doing the same types of activities before bed i.e. have a bath, brush your teeth, read a story, go to sleep.

Helpful Hint: Have your child help you remember the bedtime routine (which job comes next) to make a fun time out of getting ready for bed. This way your child feels like he's making the decisions.

Helpful Hint: Don't insist on your child sleeping, you could say for example: "It's alright if you don't want to sleep - but you must lay here in bed and just rest quietly". I think you'll soon find your child sleeping on his own.

PREDICTABLE BOOK LIST

Predictable books are books which follow a particular pattern of language. The stories have alot of repetition and children become familiar with the books quickly and can therefore read along with you. They take great pride in that they can "read" their own books. Great for beginning readers.

Alain. *One Two Three Going to Sea*
Aliki. *Go Tell Aunt Rhody*
Aliki. *My Five Senses*
Asch, Frank. *Monkey Face*
Balian, Lorna. *The Animal*
Balian, Lorna. *Where in the World is Henry?*
Barchas, Sarah E. *I Was Walking Down the Road.*
Baum, Arline and Joseph. *One Bright Monday Morning*
Becker, John. *Seven Little Rabbits*
Beckman, Kaj. *Lisa Cannot Sleep*
Bellah, Melanie. *A First Book of Sounds*
Boone, Rose, and Mills, Alan. *I Know an Old Lady*
Brand, Oscar. *When I First Came to this Land*
Brandenberg, Franz. *I Once Knew a Man*
Brown, Marcia. *The Three Billy Goats Gruff*
Brown, Margaret Wise. *Four Fur Feet*
Brown, Margaret Wise. *Goodnight Moon*
Brown, Margaret Wise. *Home for a Bunny*
Brown, Margaret Wise. *Where Have You Been?*
Carle, Eric. *The Grouchy Ladybug*
Carle, Eric. *The Very Hungry Caterpillar*
Carle, Eric. *The Mixed Up Chameleon*
Charlip, Remy. *Fortunately*
Charlip, Remy. *What Good Luck! What Bad Luck!*
Cook, Bernadine. *The Little Fish That Got Away*
de Regniers, Beatrice Schenk. *Catch a Little Fox*
de Regniers, Beatrice Schenk. *May I Bring A Friend?*
de Regniers, Beatrice Schenk. *Willy O'Dwyer Jumped in the Fire*
de Regniers, Beatrice Schenk. *How Joe the Bear and Sam the Mouse Got Together*
de Regniers, Beatrice Schenk. *The Little Book*
Domanska, Janina. *If All the Seas Were One Sea*
Duff, Maggie. *Jonny and His Drum*
Duff, Maggie. *Rum Pum Pum*
Emberley, Barbara. *Simon's Song*
Ets, Marie Hall *Elephant in a Well*
Ets, Marie Hall. *Play with Me*
Flack, Marjorie. *Ask Mr. Bear*
Galdone, Paul. *Henny Penny*
Galdone, Paul. *The Three Bears*
Galdone, Paul. *The Three Billy Goats Gruff*
Galdone, Paul. *The Three Little Pigs*
Ginsburg, Mirra. *The Chick and The Duckling*
Greenberg, Polly. *Oh Lord, I Wish I was a Buzzard*

Hoffman, Hilde. *The Green Grass Grows All Around.*
Hutchins, Pat. *Good-Night Owl.*
Hutchins, Pat. *Rosie's Walk.*
Hutchins, Pat. *Titch*
Keats, Ezra Jack. *Over in the Meadow*
Kent, Jack. *The Fat Cat*
Klein, Leonore. *Brave Daniel*
Kraus, Robert. *Whose Mouse Are You?*
Langstaff, John. *Frog Went A-Courtin'*
Langstaff, John. *Oh, A-Hunting We Will Go*
Langstaff, John. *Gather My Gold Together: Four Songs for Four Seasons*
Laurence, Ester. *We're Off to Catch a Dragon*
Lexau, Joan. *Crocodile and Hen*
Lobel, Anita. *King Rooster, Queen Hen*
Lobel, Arnold. *A Treeful of Pigs*
Mack, Stan. *10 Bears in My Bed*
Mayer, Mercer. *If I Had . . .*
McGovern, Ann. *Too Much Noise*
Memling, Carl. *Ten Little Animals*
Moffett, Martha. *A Flower Pot is Not a Hat*
Peppe, Rodney. *The House That Jack Built*
Polushkin, Maria. *Mother, Mother, I Want Another*
Preston, Edna Mitchell. *Where Did My Mother Go?*
Quackenbush, Robert. *She'll Be Comin' Round the Mountain*
Rokoff, Sandra. *Here is a Cat.*
Scheer, Jullian, and Bileck, Marvin. *Rain Makes Applesauce*
Scheer, Jullian, and Bileck, Marvin. *Upside Down Day*
Sendak, Maurice. *Where the Wild Things Are*
Shaw, Charles B. *It Looked Like Spilt Milk*
Shulevitz, Uri. *One Monday Morning*
Skaar, Grace. *What Do the Animals Say?*
Sonneborn, Ruth A. *Someone is Eating the Sun*
Spier, Peter. *The Fox Went Out on a Chilly Night*
Stover, JoAnn. *If Everybody Did*
Tolstoy, Alexzi. *The Great Big Enormous Turnip*
Welber, Robert. *Goodbye, Hello*
Wildsmith, Brian. *The Twelve Days of Christmas.*
Wolkstein, Diane. *The Visit*
Wondriska, Willian. *All the Animals Were Angry*
Zaid, Barry. *Chicken Little*
Zemach, Harve. *The Judge*
Zemach, Margot. *The Teeny Tiny Woman*
Zolotow, Charlotte. *Do You Know What I'll Do?*

Body awareness

FINGERPLAYS AND SONGS

Open Them, Shut Them

Open them, shut them, open them, shut them *(stretch fingers and make fists)*
Give them a little clap *(clap your hands)*
Open them, shut them, open them, shut them *(stretch fingers and make fists)*
Lay them in your lap *(lay hands on your lap)*

Creep them, creep them, creep them, creep them *(walk fingers up to your chin from lap)*
Right up to your chin
Open wide your little mouth *(open your mouth)*
But do not let them in *(hide fingers behind back)*

A Poem About Me

I have two eyes to see with *(point to eyes)*
I have two feet to run *(run in place)*
I have two hands to clap with *(clap hands)*
And a nose I have but one *(point to nose)*
I have two ears to hear with *(point to ears)*
A tongue to say good-bye
(point to tongue then wave good-bye)
I have a waist that I can bend
(place hands on waist and bend)
And ten fingers that can fly
(put hands in the air and flutter fingers)

Tall and Small

Here is a giant who is tall, tall, tall *(stand tall)*
Here is an elf who is small, small, small *(slowly sink to the floor)*
The elf who is small, will try, try, try *(rise slowly)*
To reach to the giant who is high, high, high *(stand tall, stretch arms high)*

I Can Place My Hands

On my head, my hands, I place *(place hands on head)*
On my shoulders, on my face *(place hands on shoulders, then face)*
On my hips and at my side *(place hands on hips and sides)*
Now behind my back they hide *(hide hands behind back)*

My Hands

This little hand is a good little hand *(show one hand)*
And this little hand is its brother *(show other hand)*
They wash and they scrub *(pretend to wash)*
And together they rub
Till one is as clean as the other *(show clean hands)*

What Can I Do?

(tune: Drunken Sailor)
What can I do with both my hands?
What can I do with both my hands?
What can I do with both my hands?
As I am growing up
Give them a clap and shake them all over
Give them a clap and shake them all over
Give them a clap and shake them all over
And I'm growing up

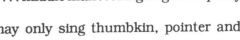

Where Is Thumbkin

(tune: Are You Sleeping)
Where is Thumbkin? (2) *(hold hands behind back)*
Here I am *(close other fingers, wave thumb)*
Here I am *(wave thumb from other hand)*
How are you this morning *(have thumbs look as if they are speaking)*
Very well I thank you *(to each other, asking how each is)*
Run and hide *(hide one hand behind back)*
Run and hide *(hide other hand behind back)*

Continue with where is pointer . . . middle man . . . ring finger . . . pinky
. . . whole family . . . .
With younger children you may only sing thumbkin, pointer and whole family.

What I Can Do

(tune: London Bridge)
I hop about on one foot (hop on one foot)
I can also hop on two (hop on two feet)
I can swing my arms around (hop and swing arms)
And wave right back to you (hop and wave)

Doing Song

(tune: Mary Had a Little Lamb) (do actions while you sing)
Reach up high to the sky
Touch your nose and then your toes
Shake your hands, while you stand
Turn around and then sit down

Body Parts

(tune: Frére Jaques)
Do you have eyes, do you have eyes (point to eyes)
Yes I do, yes I do (nod your head)
Yes I have two eyes, yes, I have two eyes (nod and point to eyes)
Cover and hide, cover and hide (cover eyes)
(continue with other body parts)

Head and Shoulders

(tune: Mary Had a Little Lamb) (point to parts of body as you sing)
Head and shoulders, knees and toes
Knees and toes, knees and toes
Head and shoulders, knees and toes
Ears, eyes, chin and nose

That's Part of Me

(tune: This is the Way) (point to body parts)
My head, my shoulders, (my knees, my toes) (3)
My head, my shoulders, my knees, my toes
That's all part of me
My eyes, my mouth, (my ears, my nose) (3)
My eyes, my mouth, my ears, my nose
That's all part of me

Bend

(tune: Skip To My Lou)
Bend to the left and bend to the right (3)
Skip around in a circle
*Sing this a couple of times then add variations such as clap, nod, hop, wave, point, etc.

Roll Your Hands

Roll your hands, roll your hands
So slowly
As slowly, as slowly as can be
Roll your hands, roll your hands
So quickly
Then put them on your head like me

My Hands

See my hands (hold up both hands)
Yes, I have two
Here are some things
My hands can do
Brush my hair (brush hair)
Wash my face (pretend to wash face)
Button my coat (button imaginary buttons)
Tie my laces (stoop to tie laces)
Throw a ball (pretend to throw a ball)
Sweep the floor (pretend to sweep)
Pick up things (stoop to pick up things)
Shut the door (pretend to shut the door)

ARTS AND CRAFTS

Body Parts Cut-Outs

Materials: catalogue or magazine
             paper
             scissors
             glue

Cut out body parts from a magazine or catalogue. Have your child put
the funny person together and glue onto a sheet of paper.

Make-Me Art

Materials: large white or brown paper
             newspaper (optional)
             paint or crayons/markers
             pencil
             buttons, yarn, pieces of material (optional)

Have child lay down on large paper and trace around his body. Use
crayon, paint, and/or markers to dress and decorate your person.
Variation: You can also glue yarn for hair, buttons for eyes, nose, etc.

Facial Parts Cut-Outs

Materials: magazine
white paper ovals
scissors
glue

Cut some face parts out of a magazine. Have your child glue the face parts onto the white paper ovals.

Hand and Footprints

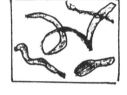

Materials: tempera paint
white paper

Dip hands into tempera paint and make hand prints. Feet prints are fun too!

Pudding Painting

Materials: pudding (colored)
paper

Use pudding to fingerpaint. Have child spread pudding using fists, knuckles, fingertips, palms, etc.

GAMES

Blindfold Game

Blindfold your child and have him touch your limbs or facial features. The child tries to identify the body part touched.

Simon Says

(2 or more)

Leader directs participant to do action by saying "Simon Says do this" then do action (lift leg, arms, touch nose, etc.) Everytime the leader says "Simon Says" he does a new action. Participant follows leaders action. The leader tries to get participant to do action without saying "Simon Says". If he is caught not saying "Simon Says" then he becomes participant and there is a new leader. Preschoolers find this game loads of fun.

✱ Musical Bodies

Children skip around the room while music is played. When the music is stopped children are to quickly stop and do as previously instructed (sit on bum, put head on floor, 1 knee on floor, etc.) Try to use as many body parts as you can. Children will get plenty of laughs from this game.

✱Friendship Relay

(4 or more)

Have children choose a partner and stand at opposite ends of a room facing each other. Give the children instructions to do something and then run back to their own sides.

1. run to each other and give your partner a handshake, then run back to your side of the room
2. run to each other and give your partner a hug,
3. twirl your partner
4. bump bums
5. slap hands
6. touch toes
7. rub heads
8. make a funny face

Be creative!

Teaching the alphabet

TEACHING THE ALPHABET

- Make alphabet letters with playdough.
- Make alphabet shapes using the body or parts of the body.
- Buy alphabet macaroni and cereal for child to use.
- Make alphabet stepping stones on indoor-outdoor carpet pieces.
- Look for letters in newspapers.
- Trace a letter on your child's back. Have her guess.
- Put sand or salt in a box and have your child draw letters.
- Trace letters in the air, on the floor, leg, etc. Use your finger, toe, knee, elbow, nose . . .
- Indent letters on styrofoam meat trays. Have child trace over them.
- Draw pictures with letters hidden in them.
- Make lacing letters on cardboard.
- Glue over letter outlines with macaroni, cereal, etc.
- Have an alphabet hunt in your house. When child finds the letters, he has to tell you what they are.
- Make a set of your child's name and the alphabet letters in his name to match.
- Help your child learn to sing the alphabet to a certain tune.
- Play a game in which you and your child face each other. The first person says "A", the opposite person says "B", and so on.
- Have child paste string to letters printed by you.
- Give young child yarn to form into letters that you call out.
- Give each child a scoop of pudding on a plate. Have the child draw a letter that you show her or call out. Great for practicing their names too!
- Have a letter of the week. Paste the letter on the fridge and everytime your child uses the fridge he'll see the letter.

Teaching Beginning Sounds

- Say initial sound of child's name (ie: Brock) Your name starts with letter B. B-B-B-B. What other things start with that sound? ball, baby, etc.
- Classify objects, pictures by first sound.
- Booklets: make an alphabet booklet, cut out pictures that start with a particular sound.
- Take a walk, find things beginning with the same sound.

Family Shapes

I am mama circle
Round like a pie
I am a baby triangle
Three sides have I
I am papa square
My sides are four
I am Uncle triangle
Shaped like a door
Cut out shapes and hold them up as your child says each shape.

Mystery Box

Children love this game.
Place the four basic shapes inside the box. Child places his hand inside the box and describes the shape that he *feels*.

Children love the mysteriousness of the mystery box and will want to play this game over and over.
Say: Here's a box
Well, what's inside?
Put your hand in
And see what you can find

Variation: After she feels the shape, she can draw her shape on a blackboard or piece of paper.

Song on Shapes

(tune: *Did You Ever See A Lassie*)
Did you ever see a circle, a circle, a circle
Did you ever see a circle
Please show me one now
Oh, Brock, Oh Brock, Oh Brock
Oh, Brock. Did you ever see a circle
Please show me one now.

Child walks over to or points to circle in the room. You must take your turn too, while your child sings.
Did you ever see a triangle? etc.

Activities:

• Talk about shapes in napkins, biscuits, cups, pail, at lunchtime, etc.
• Give your child a stencil of a shape made out of construction paper or cardboard. Have your child trace the outline of the shape with his hand. Trace the outside of the shape onto another piece of paper with a pencil or crayon.
• Make pictures using shapes. Cut out the 4 basic shapes from construction paper and have child glue them onto another piece of paper, making a picture.
• Name a shape and have your child think of all the things he can that are that shape.

Number Activities

• Make "Funny Number Man" pictures by tracing around large number patterns. Add arms, legs, facial features, etc.

• Make cookie dough numerals from any dough recipe. Make stiff cookie dough by adding 1/2 cup extra flour. Bake in the usual fashion.
• Child prints large numeral and covers with split pea seeds, alphabet macaroni, or sand. This makes "feely" letters. Also, can cover with poppy seeds, styrofoam packing materials.
• Make numerals with pipe cleaners.

The Donut Monster Game

Your child will love playing this game over and over again.
Materials: Give your child a paper cup or napkin with ten or fifteen cheerios or fruit loops.

Mom/Dad	Child
"This is the story abut a donut monster. He loved to eat donuts. In this story you are going to be the donut monster. Who is going to be the donut monster?"	"Me." "I am."
"One bright spring morning the donut monster went out to play marbles. All at once he saw two donuts sitting on a napkin. Show me what happened."	Your child should take out two cheerios and place them on the napkin.
"Boy am I hungry," said the monster and he gobbled up one of the donuts. *(look at the child expectantly)*	Child eats one of the cheerios.
"And that left how many donuts?"	"One"
"As he walked around he found two other donuts. How many donuts can he see now?"	Child puts out 2 or more and says - 3
"It didn't take the donut monster very long to pop one donut in his mouth and eat it."	Child eats one cheerio and says . . .
"That left . . . "	"Two"
"The donut monster was still hungry so he ate one more donut, and that left . . . "	Child eats one more and says, "One"

Continue to add and subtract until all the cheerios are eaten. Tell the story over and over again to reinforce number concepts at different levels. Let your child improvise and tell you the story.

Teaching Your Child To Print Numbers

Use these little verses when teaching your child to print.

1 A straight line down is lots of fun,
Because it makes, the number one.

2 Around and back,
On the railroad track . . . two, two, two.

3 Around a tree, around a tree,
Makes a very pretty three.

4 Down and over, then down some more,
That's the way we make a four!

5 Big old five goes down and around,
Put a flag on top, and see what you've found.

6 Down to a loop
A six rolls a hoop!

7 Across the sky and down from heaven
That's the way we make a seven.

8 We make an S but do not wait
We climb back up and there's an eight.

9 A loop at the top and then a line
Makes a very handsome nine.

10 It's easy to make a one and an 0
Ten, is all of your fingers, you know.

Practise in sand or salt.

Helpful Hint: Give your child crayons or large pencils when learning how to print. Don't let him use pens or fine tipped markers.

Parents can help their children prepare for kindergarten

- Try to develop good rich concepts about the everyday world in which we live.
- Give your child ample opportunity to do creative art, to cut and paste and model with clay and plasticine.
- Give your child ample opportunity to listen to good music and respond to rhyme.
- Give your child an opportunity to learn nursery rhymes, finger plays and a variety of poems.
- Set aside a time everyday to read to your child.
- Take your child to as many worthwhile places in the community as possible: zoo, park, farm, library.
- Teach your child his full name, his parent's name, his phone number, his address and the city in which he lives.
- Make opportunities for your child to play with others his own age.
- Establish habits of having him pick up and put away his toys, books and clothing.
- Help your child realize that he is one of a family group and that there are times when others need more attention than he does.
- Provide opportunities for your child to develop and carry out his own ideas in his play, and to participate in family group activities, such as daily tasks and responsibilities.
- Teach him to put on and take off his jacket, boots or shoes.
- Help your child learn safety rules in crossing streets.
- Create a happy attitude toward school so that your child anticipates with pleasure his first school experience.

RECIPES

Melted Crayons

Accumulate all your childs broken pieces of crayon, and make one large crayon.

Place wax paper in muffin tins and place broken crayons in each tin. Place in the oven on low heat and when the crayons have melted completely, set them aside to harden.

Soapsuds Picture

1/2 cup	dry detergent	125 ml
	or	
1 capful	liquid detergent	
2 tsp.	liquid starch	10 ml
	brown paper	
	paints or food coloring	

Beat detergent and starch in a bowl until thick as frosting. If you want different colors, put mixture into different jars and add colour. Dip colored soapsuds from jar with finger and paint on brown paper. If soapsuds thicken, add more starch and beat it into the mixture. Leave picture down until dry.

Fingerpaint

3 tbsp.	sugar	45 ml
1/2 cup	cornstarch	125 ml
2 cups	cold water	500 ml
	coloring	
	detergent	

Mix sugar and cornstarch together. Stir in water. Cook over low heat 2-3 minutes. Put in 4-5 pots and add color and bits of detergent.

Glitter-Goop

1 cup	flour	250 ml
1 cup	salt	250 ml
1 cup	water	250 ml
	food coloring	

Mix together in order. Put in squeeze type bottles (i.e. shampoo.) Squeeze on heavy paper or meat trays.

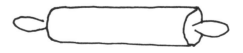

Bubble Blowing

1/3 cup	liquid detergent (Joy works best)	85 ml
2/3 cup	water	170 ml

Mix together. Make a blower by bending a wire into a circle leaving a long end, or use a plastic bubble blower. (Twist ties from garbage bags work great!) Dip the blower into the solution and blow.

Dough It

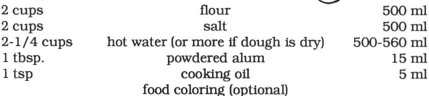

2 cups	flour	500 ml
2 cups	salt	500 ml
2-1/4 cups	hot water (or more if dough is dry)	500-560 ml
1 tbsp.	powdered alum	15 ml
1 tsp	cooking oil	5 ml
	food coloring (optional)	
	tempera paint (optional)	

In a bowl mix the flour, salt, water, and alum. Add the cooking oil and some food coloring. Knead for 5 minutes until dough is smooth. Model into flat shapes or three-dimensional objects. Let your creations dry for several days. You may paint them when hardened. (see photograph)

Be sure to pinch dough together so that it will stick when dry.

Dough It Again

Edible.

1 pkg.	dry yeast	1 pkg.
1-1/2 cups	warm water	375 ml
1	egg	1
1/4 cup	honey	60 ml
1/4 cup	shortening	60 ml
1 tsp.	salt	5 ml
5 cups	flour (approx.)	1-1/4 litres
	shellac (optional)	

Sprinkle dry yeast into very warm water. Stir until yeast is dissolved. Mix in the egg, honey, shortening and salt. Stir in flour a little at a time until you have a ball of dough that's not too sticky to handle. Knead dough about 5 minutes. Shape dough on cookie sheet into one large figure or many small ones. Make only flat figures. Cover the sculpture with a towel and let it rise in a warm place for 25 minutes. Bake about 20 minutes or until golden brown at 350°F. Brush melted butter over sculpture to give shiny effect. If you don't want to eat your sculpture, you can shellac it after it cools. It will keep for a long time. (see photograph)

Playdough

Bring to boil until dissolved.

2 cups	water	500 ml
1/2 cup	salt	125 ml
	food coloring	

Then add:

2 tbsp.	salad oil	30 ml
2 tbsp.	powdered alum	30 ml

Mix into above solution while hot.

2 cups	flour	500 ml

Knead for 5 minutes while still warm. The playdough will keep up to two months in a plastic bag.

Clay for Creative Play

1 cup	cornstarch	250 ml
2 cups	baking soda	500 ml
1-1/4 cups	cold water	310 ml

Stir the cornstarch and soda together in a saucepan. Mix in the water and cook over medium heat stirring constantly until mixture reaches a slightly moist, mashed potato consistency. Turn out onto a plate. Cover with a damp cloth. When the clay is cool enough to handle, knead it like dough until it is plastic and easy to use. The clay is now ready to use, but you can store it tightly covered for later use. To dry your creations, leave at room temperature in a safe place. Turn occasionally. Small objects will dry overnight and large objects will dry in a couple of days. When the creations dry, have the children decorate them with water colors, poster paints, felt tip pens, or leave them plain.

Suggestions for gifts: candlesticks, paperweights, jewellery, wall plaques.

Note: clay is not edible.

T HINGS
O SAVE

Things to Save

baby food jars
baking cups
bottle caps
buttons
cotton scraps and ribbon
cotton balls
drinking straws
egg cartons
ivory soap
jar lids
macaroni
magazines
newspaper
nylons
paper bags
paper plates
pine cones
plastic containers
popcorn kernels
popsicle sticks
seeds of all kinds
spools
string
styrofoam meat trays/cups
tin foil
tissue paper
toilet paper rolls/paper towel rolls
yarn

Things to Buy

crayons
construction paper
gummed seals
Mactac
markers
paints and paint brushes
pipe cleaners
scissors
styrofoam balls
tape
white paper

INDEX

INDEX

Share your enjoyment by giving someone

The Best in Kids

Please send me _____ copies of **The Best in Kids** at $12.95 per book plus $1.00 each for postage and handling, plus 7% G.S.T. Total is $14.93

Enclosed is $_____

Name: _____

Street: _____

City: _____ **Province:** _____

Postal Code: _____
please make cheques payable to:
Western Extension College
Box 110
Saskatoon, Saskatchewan, Canada
S7K 3K1

Use "The Best In Kids" *as a fund-raiser*
for your organization
For further information contact:

Western Extension College
Box 110
Saskatoon, Saskatchewan, Canada
S7K 3K1
Phone: (306) 373-6399

or simply mail this card with your name, address and phone number.

_____

_____

_____

_____

_____

POSTAGE

Mail to:

**Western Extension College
Educational Publishers
Box 110
Saskatoon, Saskatchewan
Canada
S7K 3K1**